THE
ANXIETY
Answer Book

THE

THE ANXIETY
Answer Book

LAURIE A. HELGOE, PhD
LAURA R. WILHELM, PhD
MARTIN J. KOMMOR, MD

SOURCEBOOKS, INC.®
NAPERVILLE, ILLINOIS

Published by Sourcebooks, Inc.
P.O. Box 4410, Naperville, Illinois   60567-4410
(630) 961-3900
fax: (630) 961-2168
www.sourcebooks.com

Library of Congress Cataloging-in-Publication Data

Helgoe, Laurie A.
   The anxiety answer book / Laurie A. Helgoe, Laura R. Wilhelm, Martin J. Kommor.
      p. cm.
   Includes bibliographical references and index.
   ISBN 1-4022-0402-7 (alk. paper)
      1. Anxiety--Popular works. 2. Anxiety--Treatment--Popular works. 3. Panic attacks--Popular works. I. Wilhelm, Laura R. II. Kommor, Martin J. III. Title.

   RC531.H44 2006
   616.85'22--dc22
                                                        2005012506

Printed and bound in the United States of America.
BG   10   9   8   7   6   5   4   3   2   1

For Barron, Bjorn, and Josh, who keep me grounded and help me soar.
—L. H.

To my family—my husband Ed, my parents Yvonne and Bob, and my sister and brother-in-law Lisa and Weston. I love you all and feel so blessed to have you in my life. Thank you for everything you have given me.
—L. W.

To Ben Kommor, who instructs and inspires me in the tender art of fatherhood.
   —M. K.

Acknowledgments

Many thanks to our editor, Bethany Brown, for her help, patience, and dedication to quality. Gratitude always to Jacky Sach, my agent. And thanks to my friends from The Writer's Village—my lifeline through the ups and downs of writing. Special thanks to my dear friends, Beth, Mimi, and Cindy, and my sisters, Julie and Becca, for just making life better.
—Laurie A. Helgoe

My deepest thanks are extended to the following individuals for their excellent teaching, mentorship, and support: Robert Beck, PhD, Thomas Ellis, PsyD, ABPP, Chris France, PhD, John Linton, PhD, ABPP, and Holly Cloonan, PhD. I also feel very privileged and grateful to have received training at the Albert Ellis Institute and the Beck Institute—the education, staff, fellow trainees, and overall experiences at each of these establishments were amazing. Additional heartfelt thanks to Shannon Froese, PhD, Natalie Shaheen, MD, Liz Moore, MA, Richard Granese, MD, and Esther Stephenson—your friendship always means so much to me, but your help with looking over book drafts was particularly appreciated!
—Laura R. Wilhelm

Many thanks to Laurie A. Helgoe, PhD, and Laura R. Wilhelm, PhD.
—Martin J. Kommor

Contents

Introduction

ANXIETY: THE ALARMING EMOTION

An alarm is sounding in your body. You feel as if danger is at hand, yet no one is chasing you, and no disaster threatens your safety. You may be worrying about something specific, or just feel concerned for no apparent reason. Either way, you know that the alarm is out of proportion with your present situation. Knowing this does not help. You are anxious.

If you suffer from anxiety, or live with someone who does, you are aware of the trouble it can cause. The anxious person feels pressed. It's hard to think clearly. She feels the need to respond, but her responses help only temporarily, if at all. She might feel yelled at from inside. Family members get tired of reassuring her, and she gets tired of trying to explain feelings she may not even understand.

Anxiety is the most common mental health complaint, and all of us have felt in its clutches at some point in our lives. Some anxiety is healthy and necessary to keep us alive; too much anxiety, however, can interfere with living well. Fortunately, we have learned a great deal about anxiety—about what makes it worse and what makes it better. *The Anxiety Answer Book* pulls this information together in an easy question-and-answer format, providing tools to help you reduce your anxiety and enjoy your life more.

Chapter 1

ANXIETY BASICS

- What is anxiety?
- What causes anxiety?
- What are the different kinds of anxiety disorders?
- How common are anxiety disorders?
- If I have problems with anxiety, does that mean I have a mental illness?
- What are the warning signs that my anxiety needs treatment?
- Can a person be hospitalized for anxiety?
- Do my genes make me more likely to have anxiety?
- Does the way I was raised make me more or less likely to be anxious?
- Will I just grow out of my anxiety if I leave it alone?
- What kinds of anxiety disorders are seen in children?
- Can physical illness or medication produce anxiety-like symptoms?
- How does alcohol affect anxiety?
- How are depression and anxiety related?
- Can anxiety make a person more likely to commit suicide?
- Can some anxiety be healthy?

What is anxiety?

Anxiety is fear without a clear threat. Whereas fear is a natural reaction to an obvious, literal threat to your physical well-being, anxiety often feels abnormal and without use or function. Imagine crossing a street and suddenly a car appears speeding in your direction. You will probably experience the following symptoms of fear:

- Your heart races
- Your breathing increases
- You may perspire
- Your mind focuses
- You are overcome by a sense of urgency to take protective action

These reactions, which happen in a split second, will hopefully spare you from an unpleasant encounter with 3,000 pounds of steel, and leave you grateful for your built-in alarm system. Anxiety, on the other hand, feels more bothersome than helpful. Compare the logic and efficiency of the fear response to these common features of anxiety:

- You may not be able to identify why you're afraid
- If you have a reason, it's not a convincing one (it may be irrational)
- The threat may be distant in the past or future
- The threat could be distant geographically
- When you don't know why you are afraid, you feel a sense of foreboding
- Because the fear lacks focus, you have more trouble finding a solution to bring closure to it.

Moreover, anxiety is self-perpetuating. The more you notice yourself feeling anxious, the more anxious you may become.

What causes anxiety?

Many factors contribute to anxiety, and several may apply in each particular case. Here's a list of the causes most often associated with the development of anxiety disorders:

Genes. Our genes set some of us up to be susceptible to problems with anxiety. If a number of your close relatives suffers from anxiety problems, you are at an increased risk for developing an anxiety disorder. You may inherit a more sensitive alarm system.

Early Life Experience. Early life events and experiences can also make us more likely to develop problems, especially if these experiences are traumatic and leave an echoing alarm in our heads. Just seeing our parents respond to events with anxiety and worry may make it more likely that we will respond the same. If your parents reinforced or rewarded anxious behavior, you may have learned that being anxious got you what you wanted.

Later Life Experience. Experiencing particularly traumatic events later in life can result in problems with anxiety over the short-run and, in some cases, for an extended period of time. Examples of this include the trauma caused by rape or war combat.

Your Thinking. Often, we are alarmed by our own thinking. Logical errors are common among people with anxiety problems, namely overestimating the danger in a situation and underestimating one's ability to cope. Anxious people may consistently overemphasize the downside of an event. They may have trouble sorting out what actually is risky in life.

Drugs and Illness. Various drugs, legal and illegal, set off the anxiety alarm, as do some medical or other psychiatric illnesses.

Conflict. Some of us become anxious when faced with troublesome dilemmas—the lesser of two evils or the greater of two goods. Such a conflict may be based in unconscious alarms (e.g., signaling a parent's disapproval) that continue to impact us as adults. This kind of cause is referred to as "psychodynamic" because it addresses the conversations, or dynamics, that occur inside us.

Brain Wiring. Our brains are "wired" with built-in alarm systems to insure we survive. Sometimes the brain structures tied to these alarm systems are built differently or function differently than usual.

Anxiety problems stem from a combination of factors. When a number of these factors come together, the anxiety disorder might be more serious. For example, someone who has family members with anxiety, suffered from and was reinforced for anxiety problems as a child, and experiences a major trauma later in life will likely have more difficulties than someone who experiences only the late-life trauma.

What are the different kinds of anxiety disorders?

The primary types of anxiety disorders include the following:

1. **Generalized anxiety disorder**, which is diagnosed for people who suffer at least six months of persistent and excessive anxiety and worry.

2. **Panic disorder** is diagnosed when a person has recurrent, unexpected panic attacks and worries about having more.

3. **Agoraphobia** is the fear of being in places or situations where escape may be difficult or embarrassing. Agoraphobia is often associated with concerns about having a panic attack.

4. **Phobias**, which include *specific phobias* and *social phobia*, are diagnosed when clinically significant anxiety occurs upon exposure to the feared object or situation, and this fear often leads to avoidance of the object or situation.

5. **Obsessive-compulsive disorder** is characterized by *obsessions*, which are intrusive thoughts and impulses (e.g., thoughts about contamination) causing significant anxiety, and *compulsions*, which are repetitive behaviors (e.g., excessive hand-washing) used to ward off that anxiety.

6. **Posttraumatic stress disorder** and **acute stress disorder** involve the re-experiencing of an extremely traumatic event.

How common are anxiety disorders?

Anxiety disorders represent the most common type of mental disorder in the United States, and affect more than 20 million Americans. In addition, about 25% of American adults has suffered intense anxiety at some point. The National Institute of Mental Health (NIMH) has useful data on anxiety disorders in American adults between the ages of 18 and 54. Here is what the NIMH studies reveal:

- About 4 million adult Americans (3.6%) are diagnosed with generalized anxiety disorder each year. Many experts believe this disorder is underdiagnosed, and estimate the prevalence to be as high as 8–9%.)
- Panic disorder affects around 1.7%, or 2.4 million, of American adults. This disorder is much higher in adolescence, and has been estimated any between 3.5% and 9% for this group. Panic disorder tends to peak at 25 years of age. One in three panic sufferers will also develop agoraphobia.
- Obsessive-compulsive disorder affects about 2.3%, or 3.3 million, of adults.
- Posttraumatic stress disorder (PTSD) occurred in about 3.6% of the population studied, although other community-based studies have found that 8% of the total adult population will be diagnosed with PTSD at some point in life. Whereas PTSD is twice as common in women as in men, it is notable that about 30% of Vietnam veterans developed PTSD after the war.
- Estimates of the prevalence of social phobia are difficult to obtain, as most people with this disorder are not diagnosed or treated unless they come in with an additional anxiety disorder. Still, the NIMH studies revealed that 5.3 million of adults, or 3.7%, are diagnosed with this disorder each year.
- Agoraphobia affects 2.2%, or 3.2 million, of American adults.

- Specific phobias were found in 4.4%, or 6.3 million, of the population studied.

Anxiety disorders are more common in women than men, and women are twice as often diagnosed with panic disorder, agoraphobia, specific phobias, PTSD, and generalized anxiety disorder. These findings may be due, in part, to the tendency for women to seek help more readily for mental health problems. Only obsessive-compulsive disorder and social phobia were found to be equally common in men and women.

If I have problems with anxiety, does that mean I have a mental illness?

First, let's clarify what a mental illness is and is not. Mental health professionals use symptom criteria from a diagnostic manual, called the *Diagnostic and Statistical Manual of Mental Disorders, Fourth Edition*, or *DSM-IV*, to determine the presence of a mental illness, now more commonly referred to as a "mental disorder." According to DSM-IV, a mental disorder is defined as "a clinically significant behavioral or psychological syndrome or pattern that occurs in an individual and that is associated with present distress or disability or with significantly increased risk of suffering, death, pain, or disability, or an important loss of freedom." Many of the disorders in the DSM-IV include anxiety as a prominent symptom. Further, introductory psychology textbooks generally recognize a mental disorder as a harmful dysfunction in which behavior becomes unusual, disturbing, unhelpful, and unjustifiable. Therefore, if your problems with anxiety seem atypical, distressing, and markedly interfere with your functioning, you may have a mental disorder. This may be the result of a variety of causes—for example, the structure of the brain, the way the brain cells chemically interact, increased stress, and learned ways of thinking and behaving.

What a mental illness is not, however, is an indication that a person has weak character or limited moral development. Unfortunately, this is the stigma we may carry around or worry about. Mental illness also does not automatically imply that the sufferer is "crazy" or of unsound mind. The truth is that most mental illnesses do not lead to a loss of one's grip on reality (psychosis). Anxiety disorders are rarely associated with psychosis, and sufferers are unlikely to appear any different than the average person.

What are the warning signs that my anxiety needs treatment?

Anxiety becomes a disorder when it *seriously impairs your ability to work, love, or play*. Excessive anxiety also takes its toll on your body. Here are some symptoms that impair functioning and signal the need for treatment:

- You become exhausted or easily fatigued.
- You have trouble thinking through standard problems like how to sequence the errands of the day.
- You are so tense that you can't experience comfort, joy, or a sense of accomplishment.
- You engage in special rituals to fend off intrusive thoughts or images.
- Your symptoms convince you that you're dying or losing your mind.
- Preoccupation with anxiety impairs your productivity.
- You dread common social situations such as going out in public, with friends, or even to work.
- You worry so much that it is difficult to fall asleep or stay asleep.
- Emotional tension leaks into your skeletal muscles, leaving you stiff, tense, and aching.

- You avoid everyday errands and responsibilities out of fear of experiencing a panic attack.

If you have trouble functioning, you may tend to worry more, and a vicious cycle is set in motion. Treatment is necessary to interrupt the cycle, provide hope, and restore functioning.

Can a person be hospitalized for anxiety?

It's possible but unlikely. Anxiety is a psychiatric disorder, so a patient with anxiety would need to be admitted to a psychiatric ward. However, most psychiatric wards only admit patients who are so psychiatrically ill that they are suicidal, homicidal, dangerously psychotic, or unable to feed or bathe themselves. Although some people with anxiety problems are actually disabled by the illness, most of these illnesses are never so severe that they meet the above criteria. When people with anxiety disorders do become that ill, it may be due to additional complications, such as the development of a major depressive disorder or a substance abuse problem. Such complications may be associated with feelings of helplessness and utter hopelessness that make suicide seem like a logical solution. Admission may be essential under those circumstances. Although less likely, hospitalization may be recommended when a doctor wants a patient observed while beginning a certain medication. While most psychiatric units only admit patients in acute distress, some private psychiatric hospitals are set up to provide intensive treatment to people with less severe problems. These hospitals are often expensive, and the services may not be covered by insurance.

Do my genes make me more likely to have anxiety?

Researchers have indeed identified a genetic component in anxiety disorders. We know this through twin studies, which provide an important key to the role of genetics. When twins—who share the same genes—are raised separately in adoptive families, the similarities that develop are likely to be genetic. So if one twin develops an anxiety disorder, we record whether the other twin also gets one. It appears that there is about a 25% chance that twins raised apart will both have an anxiety disorder. In order for this chance to be significant, it needs to be higher than the average stranger's chance of developing an anxiety disorder, and this figure is. Findings show that about 10% of the general population will have an anxiety disorder at some time in their lives. So, the twin studies provide some evidence of a genetic component. However, if the whole cause of anxiety were genes, then twins raised separately would both develop anxiety disorders 100% of the time. Obviously, genes are not the only factor involved.

It seems that anxiety disorders are caused by a combination of genetic and environmental influences. Posttraumatic stress disorder (PTSD) is a good example. The trauma is the experience that triggers the anxiety, but genetic factors may help explain why only certain individuals exposed to similar traumatic events develop full-blown PTSD. For some people, a life-threatening experience may lead certain brain cells to communicate differently with neighbor cells, and an illness may ensue. In contrast, other individuals may not be as biologically susceptible to the emotional impact of a life-threatening event and may recover more easily.

Does the way I was raised make me more or less likely to be anxious?

The way you were raised can certainly influence your anxiety level as an adult. Other factors, such as your biological make-up and your personality style, can also either buffer or amplify your parents' influence. In general, if your parents were calm themselves, provided consistent limits and feedback, and expressed trust and confidence in your capacities, you are likely to be less anxious. Here are some ways parenting can contribute to anxiety.

- If you were exposed to many terrifying or frightening situations and had little opportunity for protection or consolation from your parents, you may be at a higher risk for anxiety problems as a child, and as an adult. Such frightening events may include threats to you or the witnessing of threats to loved ones.
- If your parents were anxious and consistently responded to life's circumstances with anxiety, you might be at risk to copy your parents' ways of doing things.
- Without realizing it, parents may also reinforce or reward their children's anxious behavior. If I want my child to stay with me and do not allow her to be curious and explore the world, I might praise her for her fearful response to any adventuresome behavior. She may learn to please me with her anxious behavior, and find that her anxiety draws attention and care.
- Another way parents increase anxiety is to add their alarm to yours. Have you noticed how young children will look up to an adult after falling? It is as if they are trying to figure out how to respond. If the parent is calm, the child assumes she's okay and keeps playing. If the parent is alarmed and yells out "oh no!" the child becomes alarmed and breaks into tears.

- Some parents may be inconsistent with their expectations and limit-setting. As children, then, we may do something that we think is okay, but have doubts lurking in the back of our minds. That lack of clarity and doubtfulness sometimes generates anxiety.

Will I just grow out of my anxiety if I leave it alone?

Some of the anxiety disorders go away without treatment. For example, an anxiety disorder may develop during a very stressful set of circumstances (loss of a job, job search, divorce, custody battle, cancer diagnosis). When the stressors are more accepted and better managed, or even resolved, the anxiety may decline. Of the diagnosed anxiety disorders, specific childhood phobias are the most likely to diminish naturally. For example, if your child is fearful of insects, storms, or the dark, keep in mind that it is common for this type of problem to subside with age. Parents benefit from understanding that children experience typical childhood fears across different age spans, but parents also need to watch for extended, extreme suffering and reduced functioning in their child. These difficulties may signal the need for professional treatment.

Some people just continue to live with anxiety until they feel like they can't cope on their own anymore and finally talk to their doctor. Other individuals let the nervousness wear them down, ultimately giving up and resigning themselves to their suffering. Research suggests that anxiety disorders can lead to depressive disorders if left untreated. Clinical depression is a particularly debilitating medical disease that requires aggressive treatment. Although you may avoid treatment due to the constraints of time and money, it is important to remember that successful treatment is available. Usually, the earlier you seek effective treatment, the better the results for your mental well-being and quality of life. Upon finding relief through meeting with trained mental health professionals, people frequently remark "I wish I would have gone in for help sooner."

What kinds of anxiety disorders are seen in children?

The following types of anxiety disorders are most likely to be found in children and adolescents:

1. Children and adolescents with **generalized anxiety disorder** tend to be overly concerned with the quality of their performance in school or sporting events, even when they are not being evaluated. They also worry about punctuality, may be obsessed with concerns about disasters, tend to redo tasks if not perfect, and look to others for approval and constant reassurance.

2. **Separation anxiety disorder** is not categorized as an anxiety disorder in the DSM-IV, but instead listed under "Disorders Usually First Diagnosed in Infancy, Childhood, or Adolescence." This disorder is diagnosed when a child exhibits uncharacteristic anxiety about separation from home or the person to whom he is most attached. In order to be diagnosed, the problem must span at least four weeks and cause significant distress or disruption in functioning.

3. Phobias diagnosed in children include **specific phobias**, or fears of certain objects or places, or **social phobia**, fear of social situations. Specific phobias are so common in children that they are not diagnosed unless they noticeably interfere with the child's functioning (e.g., refusal to go outside due to the fear of encountering a dog). Social phobia is tricky to diagnose in children because they often do not have much control over their exposure to social situations. Given that children frequently have anxiety about interactions with adults, a diagnosis of social phobia requires that the phobic response occur in peer settings,

also. Children may express this phobia through clinging, crying and tantrums, "freezing," or not speaking.

4. Children with **obsessive-compulsive disorder (OCD)** exhibit features similar to adults with this disorder, although compulsive behaviors in children can be confused with symptoms of attention deficit/hyperactivity disorder. Some experts believe that OCD is more common among children than asthma. OCD in children may be exhibited through a child's preoccupation with lucky or unlucky numbers, having parents check to make sure things are clean, needing things to be arranged in a certain order, hoarding, or constantly asking for reassurance.

5. **Posttraumatic stress disorder** in a child may become evident through reports of nightmares and repeating of the trauma through play.

6. While not common in childhood, **panic disorder** is often first diagnosed in late adolescence.

Can physical illness or medication produce anxiety-like symptoms?

Anxiety-like symptoms can be associated with a variety of illnesses, as well as various medications. It is essential to rule out possible physical causes before concluding that you have an anxiety disorder. As you will note several times throughout this book, we recommend a comprehensive medical evaluation if you are struggling with ongoing problems with anxiety. The description below provides some information about how physical and medical influences are related to anxiety symptoms.

The conditions of hyperthyroidism and hypoglycemia can produce anxiety-like symptoms. People with hyperthyroidism have persistent increases in heart rate, whereas psychiatric anxiety produces transient and periodic rises in heart rate. It is common to have a fine tremor with hyperthyroidism. Other classic symptoms include bulging eyes and a neck goiter, though neither is always present. Thyroid dysfunction is also found in people with generalized anxiety disorder and panic disorder—keep in mind that thyroid screening is very important! Hypoglycemia stems from plummeting blood sugar levels and is frequently associated with a strong sense of anxiety. This distress may be quickly relieved by drinking a sweetened beverage.

Of course, someone experiencing an acute heart attack will report terrible anxiety and often will be sweating profusely. He may also complain of a crushing pain in his chest as if an elephant is standing on him. Other medical problems that look like anxiety disorders include: mitral valve prolapse (heart murmur), hyperparathyroidism (a condition that results in elevated calcium levels in the blood), cardiac arrhythmias, coronary insufficiency, pheochromocytoma (tumor of the adrenal gland), true vertigo, drug withdrawal, and alcohol withdrawal. Women also frequently report anxiety-like symptoms when they are beginning and going through menopause.

Many medicines produce anxiety-like symptoms, as a result of either use or discontinuation of the medicine. Nervousness can be a side effect of medications that facilitate breathing for people with asthma or chronic obstructive pulmonary disease. Some decongestants produce restlessness, as do some over the counter "anti-appetite" pills for weight loss. Caffeine is a stimulant, and it can make people nervous and jittery. Other very powerful stimulants include cocaine and amphetamines. Any stimulant can result in your feeling shaky or "revved up," including nicotine. If someone is physiologically dependent on alcohol, benzodiazepines, or barbiturates and suddenly stops using them, he may go into a serious withdrawal syndrome that includes anxiety symptoms. A person going through withdrawal is medically at risk, and if that individual has other physical illnesses, serious medical attention is crucial.

How does alcohol affect anxiety?

Alcohol interacts with anxiety in many ways. The occasional use of alcohol in moderate amounts is notorious for lessening anxiety and functioning as a social lubricant. Inhibitions and anxiety-related social restraints are loosened up. Many of the same brain cell mechanisms that allow anxiety-reducing medications (e.g., benzodiazepines) to work are the same ones that allow alcohol to calm us. Unfortunately, these benefits can quickly be outweighed by the downsides of alcohol use, including:

1. Alcohol works on many other areas of the brain, adding poor balance, impaired memory, impaired judgment, and difficulty with analytical thinking to the list of its actions. These impairments can leave us feeling vulnerable and anxious.
2. While we may feel calmed as we drink, anxiety can come rushing back in the morning, along with added concerns about the evening's indulgence.
3. The frequent use of alcohol can lead to a deep sense of sadness and, in some people, panic attacks.
4. If a person becomes addicted to alcohol, she may feel quite anxious and agitated when she stops drinking. This withdrawal syndrome is part of the reason the addict keeps drinking in spite of obvious (to others) and serious problems it causes the person.

How are depression and anxiety related?

It is common for depression and anxiety to co-occur. People often ask which comes first, the anxiety or the depression. There is no clear answer to this question. These emotional difficulties are bi-directional. For many people, the more depressed they feel, the more anxious they get; the more anxious they get, the more depressed they feel; and it becomes a vicious cycle. Here are some ways that anxiety can contribute to depression:

- **Through self-talk.** If a woman is suffering from panic attacks and telling herself "I'm weak...I should be able to get over this...There is something wrong with me," that kind of talk is going to lower her mood. Now, instead of just struggling with the panic attacks, she is also depressed.
- **Through avoidance of normal daily activities.** The more people avoid their family or friends, their jobs, and tasks they enjoy, the less fulfillment they experience. A man who stays home from work, for example, can feel a temporary sense of safety. The problem is that he is stuck in his house all day without the chance to have rewarding interactions with coworkers and opportunities to feel like he is accomplishing something. So, at the end of the day he may have succeeded in not having a panic attack by staying at home, but he now may be telling himself "I'm useless, I did nothing all day, I can't even manage my job anymore." The avoidance, and then the thoughts about it, can lead to depression.

Depression can also increase anxiety. It causes people to overestimate the risk of doing anything outside their home and to underestimate the benefits. When struggling with depression, individuals commonly think, "I can't do what I need to do, it's no use, why bother? There's no point, I don't really care about those things anyway." If you are feeling really depressed, isolating and withdrawing seem like the best things to do. For example, after a poor night's sleep, you might decide to stay home from work so you don't have to get out of bed. At the time, that decision feels good. Later in the day, however, you might start thinking "Oh no…I've missed work again…That's three days now…I'm so behind I'll never catch up…What if I get fired?" Having not performed the required activities can actually lead people to become really scared about what the consequences are going to be, which can increase the likelihood of a problem with anxiety.

Can anxiety make a person more likely to commit suicide?

Whereas fleeting thoughts of suicide are not uncommon, frequent, determined thoughts about ending one's life are a serious concern and need attention. Studies reveal that people with anxiety disorders often suffer from depression as well, and a sense of hopelessness associated with depression is the most likely reason someone contemplates taking his life. People who believe their circumstances will never improve are more likely to kill themselves than those who have some inkling of hope. And, hopelessness by definition is not based on clear, accurate thinking. Hopelessness assumes that a person knows for certain what the future holds—this is not possible.

Each year in the United States, about 10 people per 100,000 will kill themselves. If someone has the diagnosis of major depressive disorder, the likelihood of committing suicide goes up to about 400 out of 100,000. This is obviously much higher than the general population. About 20% of people with either panic disorder or social phobia *unsuccessfully* attempt to take their lives. If they are also depressed, they are more likely to go through with suicide.

Other risk factors associated with a completed suicide include:

- Being male
- Age—the older, the higher the risk
- Lack of a life partner
- Chronic illness
- Alcohol abuse
- Having a suicide plan
- Having access to a means to carry out the suicide
- Lacking a reason not to follow through
- Previous attempts and rehearsals

If you are having recurring thoughts of suicide, contact a mental health professional for help. If you feel in immediate danger of hurting yourself, call 911. Professionals and family members should realize that people who say they are suicidal are more likely to attempt it. Access to means, such as guns or pills, should be eliminated. The suicidal person may need to be in a safe place like a psychiatric hospital. If that is not possible, she should have someone around her during the risk period. The good news is that depression is very treatable through medications and/or psychotherapy. If the illness is treated and the suicidal person can see some hope, most suicidal impulses pass.

Can some anxiety be healthy?

Anxiety is considered healthy when it motivates us to take action in the name of accomplishment. Just like a good alarm clock, anxiety can signal that it's time to act. If a person gets anxious about completing a report or studying for an exam, she will take action to decrease the anxiety. The anxiety reduction she experiences is rewarding, and gives her something to look forward to the next time she has a project to complete. If the anxiety is too intense, however, it may interfere with task completion and instead lead to avoidance.

Keep in mind that anxiety at low levels is a completely natural response to new challenges and situations. A manageable level of anxiety can be an asset, serving as a motivator for change and improvement and making us more alert and attentive. An example of this is when an actor prepares to go on stage. As long as the anxiety is not excessive, the adrenaline surge can give the actor the extra boost he needs to shine.

As you read this book, you may benefit from remembering that emotions are not all-or-nothing phenomena—they occur in levels or degrees, just like a thermometer reflects temperatures in degrees. Given a particular circumstance, what would you consider a manageable level of anxiety? None (zero) is often unrealistic and maybe even impossible. Remember that there is a difference between healthy concern and excessive anxiety. Decreasing your level of anxiety usually involves thinking in a more balanced way and facing your fears instead of avoiding them.

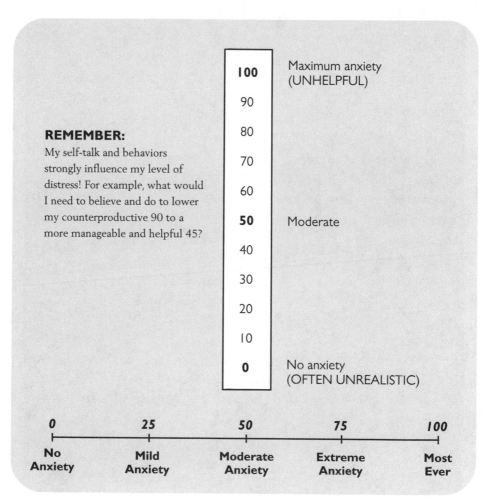

100 Maximum anxiety (UNHELPFUL)

90

80

70

60

50 Moderate

40

30

20

10

0 No anxiety (OFTEN UNREALISTIC)

REMEMBER:

My self-talk and behaviors strongly influence my level of distress! For example, what would I need to believe and do to lower my counterproductive 90 to a more manageable and helpful 45?

0	*25*	*50*	*75*	*100*
No Anxiety	**Mild Anxiety**	**Moderate Anxiety**	**Extreme Anxiety**	**Most Ever**

Chapter 2

WHAT ABOUT STRESS?

- Is stress the same thing as anxiety?
- What creates stress?
- How does stress affect my body?
- What will happen if I don't deal with the obstacles that create stress?
- What are some healthy lifestyle changes I can make to reduce stress?
- Can you explain how different people cope under stress? What is optimal?

Is stress the same thing as anxiety?

These two words are often used interchangeably. Stress implies external pressure, whereas anxiety describes an internal experience. Nevertheless, we commonly say we "have stress" or are "stressed," thus implying an internal experience as well. Perhaps the difference is that anxiety often feels unreasonable—to the sufferer as well as to others. A person may feel anxious without knowing why, or in response to a concern he knows is not significant. Stress, on the other hand, may be perceived as more reasonable, and viewed as a direct response to challenging life circumstances. Some people might say that stress is more "normal" or natural and define anxiety as more atypical or harmful.

Regardless of the word used, stress and anxiety usually involve similar physical sensations. These include muscle tension, stomach discomfort, headache, heart pounding, and a general sense of foreboding, to name a few. In response to work deadlines, relationship conflicts, or money problems, we might notice ourselves feeling easily frustrated and impatient. Worry may interfere with sleeping, and we might be more irritable. These uncomfortable feelings may improve with learning better ways to cope with stressors. Otherwise, a person may be at risk for developing stress-related illnesses, such as irritable bowel syndrome and chronic tension headaches.

Diagram (opposite):
As you can see, the same stimulus can produce different emotions and behaviors—the key is your beliefs about the stimulus!

What creates stress?

The answer to this question will be different depending on the therapist's way of looking at problems. We will look at the causes of stress from two major points of view, cognitive-behavioral and psychodynamic.

Cognitive-Behavioral Explanation: When asked about sources of stress, people often cite certain life events or situations. These might include catastrophic events (house fire, hurricane, flood), life changes (marriage, divorce, death of a loved one), or everyday hassles (difficulties at work, hectic schedule, car problems).

However, no matter what the event or situation associated with stress, it is more likely our interpretation of the event and our coping abilities that determine our level of stress. For instance, if one tells herself "I can't stand this awful work stress, I'll never make it through," she may experience a greater degree of distress than someone who

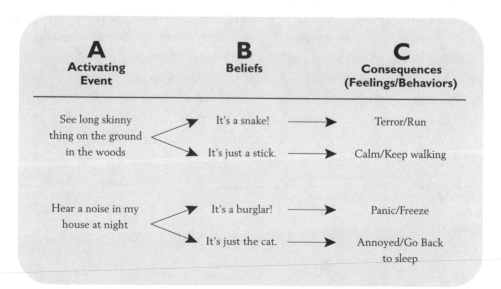

tells herself, "It's been a fairly hectic day, but I can cope with it by relaxing this evening." Even if one views an event as quite negative or stressful, her perceived ability to cope with this situation can greatly reduce the degree of distress she experiences and increase the likelihood of responding adaptively.

Psychodynamic Explanation: Stress is a sense of tension that comes from the clash of opposing "forces." On the one hand, I want to do something, or feel I *should* do something. Alternately, perhaps I want something *not* to happen, or I feel it shouldn't happen. Then come opposing **outside forces**—*they* have a different idea than what I want or feel obligated to do, and **inside forces**—*I* oppose what I want or feel obligated to do. The tension between these forces creates stress.

Here is an example. Let's say I'm a business student assigned to complete a finance project with a classmate. My class grade depends on my performance and that of my classmate. Given that my project partner tends to under-perform, I see him as an obstacle to my good evaluation. My partner shrugs off my concerns about our grade, and other students say I am a jerk if I report him to the professor. I am shy and hate to confront people. So, the obstacles I face include the project partner, my peers' code of ethics, and my own shyness and aversion to confrontation. These obstacles create friction or stress. The system is in conflict, and harmony is in short supply.

How does stress affect my body?

We have an inborn alarm system or "fight-or-flight" response that mobilizes us to stay and defend ourselves when faced with a threat, or remove ourselves from a stressful situation as a protective mechanism. This was especially helpful in our cave ancestors' days. This automatic response creates significant arousal in many biological systems, including increased heart rate, blood pressure, blood sugar, and stress hormones such as epinephrine. These responses are controlled by various body structures, including the hypothalamus, pituitary gland, and adrenal glands.

Although we are unlikely to face the same stressors as our cave ancestors these days, there may be times when equally threatening events activate us (e.g., a fast approaching car, a fire alarm). Therefore, our internal alarm system can be quite adaptive at times. However, when we are exposed to persistent stress (e.g., constant work stress) and our alarm system remains activated, our minds and bodies pay the price. We must be able to adequately cope, rest, and relax in order to continue facing our normal daily stressors. Otherwise, along with our emotional health, our physical health can diminish significantly.

If your body is in a constant state of stress arousal, you may experience problems such as hypertension, cardiac arrhythmia, difficulty sleeping, gastrointestinal upset, headaches, muscle tension, and back pain. In addition, continued stress may affect the body via unhealthy habits to cope with stress, such as overeating, smoking, frequent alcohol consumption, or drug use. Over the long-term, the body can end up in a state of dysregulation, which may increase risks of chronic and serious illness such as heart disease or cancer. Therefore, it is essential for us to learn and apply effective ways of managing stress on a regular basis.

What will happen if I don't deal with the obstacles that create stress?

The stress will need to find an outlet, and here are some ways psychodynamic theory suggests this could happen:

- You may displace your aggravation onto someone else. You might pick fights with peers, friends, loved ones, or the dog. When we get others to play out our inner problems, we are acting out the stress. This can result in marital or family problems or alienation from friends or coworkers.
- You may project your helplessness onto someone else. Rather than acknowledging that you feel stressed, you might treat others as if they are stressed, caring for friends or family beyond what is needed. This, of course, can add to your stress and result in a vicious cycle.
- You may somatize your stress, or experience your stress as a physical ailment. Focusing on bodily symptoms may feel like an easier way to receive care and support from others. Stress can also directly contribute to physical discomfort (e.g., through increased muscle tension or sleep loss).
- You may feel burned out and get depressed.
- You may turn to drinking and drug use.
- Your work performance may suffer. You might make more mistakes or forget things that result in more job-related difficulties.

What are some healthy lifestyle changes I can make to reduce stress?

Some helpful strategies include good sleep habits, proper diet, regular exercise, relaxation techniques, meditation, yoga, and developing strong social support. Incorporating healthy habits into your day is invaluable!

Practice viewing stressors in more realistic ways instead of in catastrophic terms. Learn to think in a more balanced and accurate manner. Some people benefit from labeling their stressors as opportunities—motivators for action, change, growth, and accomplishment.

Draw on your religious or spiritual tradition for comfort and strength. Many traditions encourage us to give over our worry, grief, guilt, and shame to a higher power—to let go.

It can be extremely helpful to have someone to go to, formally or informally, for counsel and comfort or to be a sounding board. This person may be anyone who listens well and can give you an objective perspective—a commuting partner, a friend you meet for lunch, a mentor, or a therapist.

It always helps to remember you are not alone in dealing with stress. Make connections with people who deal with similar stressors and share encouragement and tips. Support groups, such as Parents without Partners, Alcoholics Anonymous, or a consultation group for service providers, can reduce isolation and provide practical help.

Can you explain how different people cope under stress? What is optimal?

People typically respond to adverse circumstances in one of four ways. Each of the four styles below, or ways of coping, has distinct advantages and disadvantages:

Which style are *you* using in the issue you're facing? As you might imagine, **Taking Responsibility** is usually the healthiest and most productive style, but it also takes the most work. The other options are easier—they generally provide *short-term gain* at the cost of *long-term pain*, and tend to keep you stuck. **Taking Responsibility**—*by developing more realistic, balanced thinking and more helpful behaviors*—is really the only style that makes a meaningful difference in your problems.

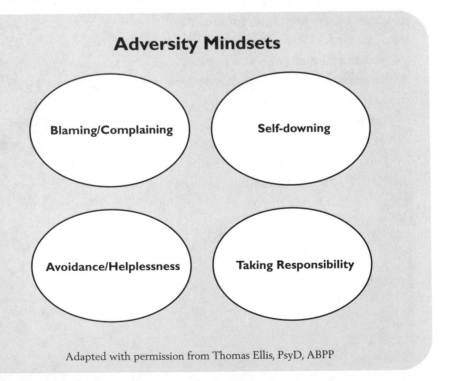

Adversity Mindsets

Blaming/Complaining

Self-downing

Avoidance/Helplessness

Taking Responsibility

Adapted with permission from Thomas Ellis, PsyD, ABPP

Chapter 3

TREATING ANXIETY WITH PSYCHOTHERAPY

- Can I get help without taking medicine?
- What types of psychotherapy are most commonly used to treat anxiety?
- How long does psychotherapy usually take?
- How much does psychotherapy cost?
- How do I know if my therapist is qualified?
- I constantly try to figure out why I'm so anxious. Do I need to know why in order to make things better?
- People tell me that I think too negatively. What's that about, and how can I change my thinking?
- I didn't expect my therapy to include work outside of sessions! Why do I need to do homework?
- When do anxious people usually come in for treatment?

Can I get help without taking medicine?

Yes. Psychotherapy is a valid alternative to medications, and has some advantages. First, you do not experience the physical side effects that may occur with medication. Second, you can develop skills and acquire tools that will help you whenever anxiety emerges. Finally, and most importantly, a successful course of psychotherapy can produce lasting change which is not dependent on the use of a chemical.

Relying on psychotherapy to alleviate anxiety does require a commitment of time and energy. Your motivation to get better is a key factor in the effectiveness of your therapy. Psychotherapy often does induce temporary distress, as it involves facing the sources of your anxiety. The difference is that you are taking charge of the anxiety rather than the other way around.

If you are considering therapy, remember that a variety of therapeutic approaches exists. These are described in more detail in the next question. Further, many therapists practice eclectically, meaning that they use elements from several approaches that they have found to be effective with their patients. Doing some preliminary investigation to find out the approach and therapist with whom you feel most comfortable working is a good idea. Further, the "fit" between the two of you is very important no matter what technique is used.

What types of psychotherapy are most commonly used to treat anxiety?

The research consistently favors cognitive-behavioral therapy (CBT) as the most effective treatment for the various anxiety disorders. Psychodynamic therapy has a long history, but less research backing. A newer therapy called Eye Movement Desensitization and Reprocessing (EMDR) remains controversial, but is recognized as a treatment option for trauma-based anxiety disorder. Group therapy has also been used extensively with trauma victims as well as socially phobic individuals. Other approaches include clinical hypnosis and marital and family therapy. Whereas numerous other therapies exist, the above are most often discussed in the literature.

Because of its relevance to anxiety disorders, we will discuss CBT in more detail here.

Cognitive-behavioral therapy focuses on changing the thoughts (cognitions) and behaviors that maintain anxiety. The "cognitive" part involves the identification and modification of irrational, unhelpful thoughts ("It's terrible!") that contribute to anxiety. Once the client learns to evaluate perceived threats more realistically, and through practice adopts more accurate beliefs ("It's inconvenient, but I can deal with it"), she can reduce her level of anxiety. An important foundation of CBT is the idea that our feelings and behaviors are not determined by actual events, but rather by our beliefs or thoughts about the events. Much of the work of CBT also focuses on addressing behaviors and providing exercises and assignments to help the client make changes in his day-to-day life (e.g., less avoidance, more pleasurable activities).

One of the most potent techniques in CBT is **exposure therapy**. This approach involves exposing the client—in gradual steps—to whatever it is that is triggering his anxiety (e.g., traumatic memory, phobic stimulus). At each step, the client's anxiety is allowed to peak and then diminish before advancing to the next step, until the client can be in the presence of the trigger with little or no anxiety. Research has consistently found exposure to be a key element in the effective treatment of anxiety.

Therapies that focus on **interpersonal relationships**, such as couples', family, and group therapy, may also be valuable. With these types of interventions, people come to better understand how to communicate clearly and resolve differences better. Individuals may also be taught some specific skills to ease anxiety in social situations.

Therapists who use a **psychodynamic** approach help you become aware of secret and forbidden wishes, as well as the hidden defenses you use to repress these wishes. This approach may take several months to years. The forbidden wishes (meaning we think punishment will happen if we think or feel or act on them) are thought to be part of all of us and to generate anxiety when we become aware of them. Psychodynamic therapists believe that we can reduce anxiety and assume more control over our decisions by reevaluating and accepting these forbidden wishes. The psychodynamic approach, which draws its support from case studies, parent-child observation, and conventional wisdom, is much less structured and thus difficult to research.

How long does psychotherapy usually take?

Psychotherapy for an anxiety disorder usually involves weekly sessions and can often be completed within a few months. Some therapies are shorter still, and others may take a year or more. The length is dependent on the type of therapy and the type of anxiety disorder, as well as the presence of complicating factors. Here are some factors that affect therapy length:

1. The cognitive-behavioral therapies are typically shorter than the psychodynamic ones. This is because cognitive-behavioral approaches focus on direct changes in thinking and behavior, whereas psychodynamic approaches take a broader approach and help resolve conflicts leading to problems.

2. The more longstanding the anxiety disorder, the longer it may take to have success.

3. If a patient has medical or additional psychiatric disorders, the therapy may take longer. When the anxiety co-occurs with a personality disorder, treatment might be more complicated and require a longer duration.

4. If consistent attendance at therapy sessions is a problem due to financial limitations, social or professional obligations, or the illness itself, the therapy may take longer.

One good predictor of therapy duration is how well the patient and the therapist get along with one another after two or three meetings. If they are comfortable with one another, the therapy is often more efficient and successful. It is also very important to develop a goal list with your therapist in the beginning stages of your meetings. What are you expecting to accomplish by attending therapy? The more specific your answer to this question, the better. A concrete goal list can serve as a roadmap for showing you what your targets are in therapy. Monitoring progress as you attend your therapy sessions is also vital.

How much does psychotherapy cost?

The costs of psychotherapy vary according to the discipline of the professional and the insurance policy held by the patient, as well as the region of the country. Usually psychiatrists (medically-trained physicians) have the highest fees, followed in sequence by doctoral-level psychologists, master's-level psychologists, counselors, social workers, and psychiatric nurses. We say *usually* because the clinician's experience and reputation also factor into the equation and can compensate for differences in education. Psychiatrists have a medical degree and can conduct physical exams, order lab tests, and prescribe medicines. Not all psychiatrists provide psychotherapy—many refer patients to other mental health professionals for this treatment. On the other hand, there are some psychiatrists who refer patients out for medication management and focus exclusively on providing psychotherapy.

Health insurance companies differ in the amount of mental health coverage they provide, so it is wise to look at your specific plan. Most policies limit the number of sessions they will pay for per year. Twenty to twenty-six appointments per year is a common number, but every policy is different. If you rely on a managed care network, you may need to choose your therapist from a list of approved providers.

Fees may range from $50 to $200 a session, where each session lasts 45 to 60 minutes. When insurance does not cover the cost of therapy, some clinicians offer what they call a "sliding fee scale," which bases your fee on your income. Other low-cost alternatives may be available, including university counseling centers, nonprofit clinics, and therapy training centers. It is always helpful to find out about your insurance coverage and your therapist's payment policies before starting treatment. This will save you any uncomfortable surprises, and help your therapy to progress more smoothly.

How do I know if my therapist is qualified?

Mental health professionals can be identified in two different ways: (1) by level of education, and (2) by type of license. The level of education is usually represented by the letters directly following the person's name, and includes the following abbreviations (average years of education *beyond college* in parentheses):

- MD: Medical Doctor (8–10 years)
- DO: Doctor of Osteopathy (8–10 years)
- PhD: Doctor of Philosophy (4–8 years)
- PsyD: Doctor of Psychology (4–6 years)
- MA: Master of Arts (2–4 years)
- MS: Master of Science (2–4 years)
- MSW: Master of Social Work (2–4 years)
- MEd or EdD: Master/Doctor of Education (2–4 or 4–6 years)
- MDiv/MMin or DDiv/DMin: Master/Doctor of Divinity/Ministry (2–4 or 4–6 years)
- BSN or RN: Psychiatric Nurse (0–4 years)

The second set of initials after the professional's name refers to the license that person holds. In order to obtain a license, professionals are required to obtain a certain number of hours of supervised experience, to demonstrate an understanding of the ethical requirements of their profession, and to pass a test showing their competence in the field. Whereas MDs and DOs do not typically code their license in a second set of initials, those who have completed psychiatry residency and board certification identify themselves as **psychiatrists**. You can ask any doctor which "boards" he or she is certified by. A doctoral degree from a graduate school (i.e., PhD) is usually required for licensure as a **psychologist**.

Here is a sampling of the license names and abbreviations associated with other professions:

- Licensed Clinical Social Worker: LISCW
- Licensed Marriage And Family Therapist: LMFT
- Licensed Professional Counselor: LPC
- Certified Pastoral Counselor: varies (check the website for the American Association of Pastoral Counselors at aapc.org).

This list does not cover every license issued to therapists. These vary by state, as do the titles and abbreviations for the license.

Beyond these quick indicators, it is up to you to find out the professional's areas of expertise and reputation, and to be honest with yourself about whether you trust and like your therapist. Usually a therapist will frame the first session or sessions as a "consultation" for the purpose of evaluating your problems as well as the "fit" between client and therapist. Sometimes people check out a few therapists before making a decision. Also, keep in mind that the "letters" after a clinician's name do not always indicate their expertise or qualification to treat a certain problem—you want to know what experience the clinician you see has in treating anxiety disorders in general, and your specific disorder in particular. Also, clinicians in supervised training programs may provide excellent service. Explore your options carefully.

I constantly try to figure out why I'm so anxious. Do I need to know why in order to make things better?

It's not surprising that you would want to understand *why* you feel so anxious. All people are information-processors—we like to comprehend the reasons behind events so that our world feels more predictable and manageable. Insight into "why" can help you identify old patterns and let them go. You could pursue an insight-oriented type of therapy (psychodynamic or psychoanalytic) and explore sources of anxiety in your personal history and relationships, which may help heal old wounds and free up energy for behavior change. The downsides to this approach are the time it takes and the cost. So, the question may really be, "How much insight do you need before making changes in your thinking and behavior?"

The alternative is to directly address the thinking and behaviors that are causing you problems (which can be done in cognitive-behavioral therapy, or CBT). This approach takes less time and asserts that, even if you completely understand the why behind your anxiety, you still need to make changes in your thinking and behaviors in order to get better.

Regarding your "why" question, we have found that people are anxious because of a *combination of factors*. Some of those factors include:

- **Biological predisposition to emotional disturbance**
- **Family history of anxiety**
- **Individual temperament or personality characteristics**
- **Social learning history** (e.g., overprotective parents; unpredictable, volatile household)
- **Environmental factors/stress** (e.g., troubled marriage, job loss, illness)
- **Thinking** (e.g., "I can't cope; I have no control; something terrible is going to happen.")

- **Behaviors** (e.g., avoiding problems, not getting adequate sleep, not speaking up for yourself, overextending yourself)

Perhaps the above list will help you identify some of the sources of your anxiety and free you to move forward with doing something about your anxiety. For many people, constantly asking "why?" is a distraction or avoidance technique that keeps them from facing the responsibility of making changes. Sometimes insight comes *after* you make changes! Ultimately, it is up to you to decide how much energy and time you want to put into exploring the "why" question. Remember, however, insight is important, but it is rarely enough for an improved quality of life.

People tell me that I think too negatively. What's that about, and how can I change my thinking?

Many people are in the habit of thinking negatively, but this habit can be altered. Diminishing negative thinking takes a willingness to question old, unhelpful, inaccurate ideas, and practice new, more helpful, accurate ones. **Rational Emotive Behavior Therapy** (REBT) and **Cognitive Therapy**, the two main foundations for cognitive-behavioral therapy, provide detailed explanations about the influence of overly negative thinking, as well as strategies for change.

REBT, developed by Albert Ellis, identifies 4 main types of irrational beliefs that all humans hold. These irrational beliefs generate extreme negative emotions and lead to more harmful behaviors. People do better when they challenge their irrational beliefs and develop more rational thinking (see chart, opposite).

Cognitive therapy, founded by Aaron Beck, also holds that all people regularly make "thinking mistakes" known as cognitive distortions. Sticking with distorted thinking tends to make feelings worse; developing more realistic, balanced thinking tends to improve emotions

Irrational Beliefs	Rational Alternatives
(lead to anxiety, panic, anger, rage, fury, and depression with less effective problem-solving)	(lead to concern, irritation, sadness, or disappointment, with more effective problem-solving)
Demandingness I should not have anxiety. The world should be fair and easy.	**Preferences** I wish I didn't have to struggle with anxiety, but I can face it. I wish the world were fair and easy, but it doesn't have to be.
Global Self/Other Ratings I'm no good. He's a jerk.	**Behavior Ratings (Not Judging the Worth of a Person)** I made a bad decision; I'm not bad. He behaved poorly during our talk.
Low Frustration Tolerance Because I don't like this, I can't stand it.	**Improved Frustration Tolerance** I don't like this, but I can stand it.
Awfulizing Because I don't like feeling anxious, that means it's awful, terrible, and horrible.	**De-awfulizing** Dealing with anxiety is a nuisance, but not horrible or awful.

and problem-solving. Here are some of the common thinking mistakes identified (source: *Cognitive Therapy: Basics and Beyond* by Judith Beck), with examples and alternatives:

All-or-Nothing Thinking: You see things in only two categories (good/bad, right/wrong, anxious/not anxious) without considering that there are "gray areas" or "in-betweens."

Being anxious means being miserable vs. *Being anxious is inconvenient.*

Catastrophizing: You assume that the worst will happen without realizing that other, less upsetting outcomes might be more likely.

I'll never learn to manage my fears vs. *I can learn to manage my fears if I work at it.*

Emotional Reasoning: You think something is true just because you feel it is true (this is actually a very strong belief that you hold and you're sure you're right even if there is no evidence for your belief).

I know he's going to break up with me vs. *He's told me he's very happy with me. There's no evidence that he wants to break up at this time.*

Mind-Reading: You assume you know what someone else is thinking even without them telling you.

They think I'm a loser vs. *I have no way of knowing what they're thinking.*

Personalization: You think you are the reason that something bad happened or someone reacted negatively without taking other more likely explanations into account.

He didn't say hello because I've upset him in some way vs. *He didn't say hello because he was distracted by his work.*

Should/Must Statements: You have a "demand" for how things should be (e.g., your behavior, someone else's behavior) and you exaggerate how bad it is if things don't go the way you expect them to.

I shouldn't be this anxious—it's awful vs. *Feeling anxious is often a hassle, but I can still enjoy my life.*

I didn't expect my therapy to include work outside of sessions! Why do I need to do homework?

Many therapists say that it is what you do between sessions that really makes the difference in how well your therapy works. If you have spent much of your life thinking negatively, for example, re-training your thoughts will also take time and practice.

Unrealistic, negative thinking is a habit. You can't just stop yourself from thinking negative thoughts. Instead it is more beneficial to learn to replace your unhelpful, untrue beliefs with more realistic and balanced thinking. Writing a new healthier "tape" for yourself requires work but pays off in the end!

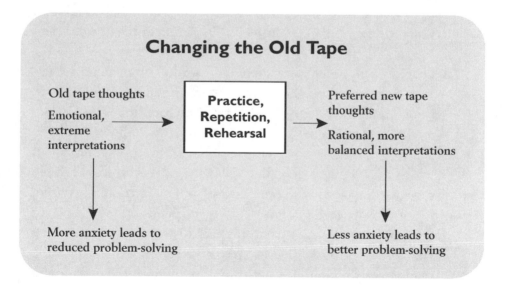

Changing the Old Tape

Old tape thoughts

Emotional, extreme interpretations

Practice, Repetition, Rehearsal

Preferred new tape thoughts

Rational, more balanced interpretations

More anxiety leads to reduced problem-solving

Less anxiety leads to better problem-solving

When do anxious people usually come in for treatment?

The point at which an anxious person seeks help often depends on the specific anxiety disorder, the person's personality, and what's going on in the environment. Here are some general observations:

1. A person having a panic attack often seeks treatment in response to the attack, thinking she is either losing her mind or having a heart attack. She will typically rush to the emergency room to have it checked out and treated, without recognizing the problem as an anxiety disorder until it is diagnosed. People with panic attacks don't go long without seeking help.

2. By contrast, people with obsessive-compulsive disorder may go years without seeking help, feeling ashamed of the problem and keeping it a secret.

3. People with generalized anxiety disorder often accept their worrying as normal. Sometimes they develop somatic symptoms—body symptoms that are manifestations of anxiety. They might feel tension headaches, upset stomachs or bowels, muscle aches, tightness in their chests, and shallow breathing, all of which may be signs of anxiety. Many people who wouldn't see a doctor for worry will see one for somatic symptoms. Often, when a worrier has a particularly difficult life challenge or dilemma, the somatic symptoms are triggered.

4. People with specific phobias may not seek treatment until the phobia clearly interferes with functioning in a more profound way. For example, someone with a fear of flying may not come in for help until he knows he must fly somewhere for his job.

5. People with social phobias can have a very troublesome time getting help, as they are fearful of doing things in front of others that will cause them humiliation.

6. Whether people seek help for acute stress disorder or posttraumatic stress disorder depends on how disruptive the symptoms are to their functioning. Just the thought of talking or thinking about the trauma again can be extremely unsettling, so people avoid seeking help. Often, PTSD sufferers initially attend treatment at the urging of loved ones—more to satisfy someone else than themselves.

Chapter 4

TREATING ANXIETY WITH MEDICATIONS

- If I suffer from anxiety, is my brain different than other people's?
- Can medication treat anxiety?
- What are the advantages and disadvantages of using these drugs?
- I've heard that benzodiazepines have many side effects. What are they? Is BuSpar a good alternative?
- Of the medications currently available for anxiety, which are having the most success?
- What are the side effects of the tricyclic and MAOI antidepressants?
- What are the side effects of the SSRI and SSRI-like antidepressants?
- My doctor mentioned that drugs like Neurontin and Inderal are being used to treat anxiety. Are they safe? What are the side effects?
- What new drugs are being studied for anxiety? How are researchers hoping to improve on current medications?
- What are the long-term side effects of medications advertised on television, like Zoloft and Paxil?
- What should I be aware of if I decide to take medication for my anxiety?
- If I stop taking an antianxiety medicine, will I get anxious again?
- To control my anxiety, will I have to take medications all my life?
- Are there any medications that are okay for someone over 70 to take for anxiety?

If I suffer from anxiety, is my brain different than other people's?

Over the years, researchers have attempted to identify brain chemicals and structures that may be involved in anxiety. Below are some of their findings.

- A chemical in the brain called **serotonin** has been linked to several human functions, such as mood, sleep, memory, and appetite. Serotonin is active in a number of areas of the brain, including the **amygdala**, a structure that controls fear and anxiety responses. Research has suggested that people with anxiety disorders may suffer from a deficiency of serotonin. This may be why a class of antidepressants called SSRIs (selective serotonin reuptake inhibitors), which increase the level of serotonin in the brain, have been successful in the treatment of anxiety disorders. The amygdala itself is currently the focus of much research on anxiety disorders, and findings suggest that emotional memories stored in this portion of the brain may contribute to phobias.

- Another promising area of continued investigation involves the brain amino acid **GABA**, short for **gamma-aminobutyric acid.** Evidence suggests that GABA may be deficient in people who suffer from anxiety. Research has shown that decreases in GABA can promote anxiety, restlessness, racing thoughts, and difficulty sleeping. By offsetting the effects of an excitement-producing brain chemical known as glutamate, GABA works to tone down brain activity and keep you calm. Benzodiazepines help boost the effect of the GABA in your brain. New research is focusing on the specific sites where GABA is received, and working to identify the functions of each of these sites. This opens up the possibility of developing medications that activate the good aspects of GABA without promoting addictive side effects.

• Modern brain technology allows us to look at differences in how brains function. Through imaging technology, we can observe blood flow to certain areas of the brain, and notice differences in the size of structures within the brain. In addition to the amygdala, researchers have focused on the **hippocampus**, a part of the brain that helps to encode information into memories. Studies have shown that the hippocampus can be up to 25% smaller in people who have undergone severe stress because of child abuse or military combat. This may explain why these individuals experience flashbacks, fragmented memories, and difficulty recalling details of the events.

It is encouraging that the more we learn about brain structure and function in people with anxiety disorders, the more we may be able to treat these concerns with better medications and therapies.

Can medication treat anxiety?

Yes, several medications can treat anxiety, and each has its own benefits and drawbacks. The type of medication used is often determined by the kind of anxiety disorder a person has.

There are two categories of effective medicines along with a few medications that are in a class by themselves. Antidepressants and benzodiazepines are the two major categories. Antidepressants, now considered a first-line medication treatment for anxiety, are divided into four categories, including: (a) the original and rarely used **tricyclics**; (b) the **monoamine oxidase inhibitors** (MAOIs); (c) the newer and more commonly used **selective serotonin reuptake inhibitors** (SSRIs); and (d) drugs similar to the SSRIs, such as Effexor.

In addition to these categories of drugs, an antianxiety medicine called BuSpar is available, and certain medications used to treat other conditions have been applied to the treatment of anxiety. Anticonvulsants, like Neurontin, are gaining popularity in their use by psychiatrists, although these medications are not well-studied as antianxiety agents. Beta-blockers, like Inderal, are another class of medications commonly utilized. Finally, antihistamines, such as Benadryl and Vistaril, are used in some cases to treat anxiety.

If you are considering medications, it is important to consult with a physician or psychiatrist who is experienced in prescribing medications *for the treatment of anxiety*. Treatment of an anxiety disorder may require a different dosage of a medication than indicated for other disorders. For example, a higher dosage of an SSRI may be needed for the treatment of obsessive-compulsive disorder than for the treatment of depression.

What are the advantages and disadvantages of using these drugs?

Let's look at each type of medication and their advantages and disadvantages:

I. Antidepressants

Examples: *Tricyclics*: Elavil, Tofranil, Norpramin, Pertofrane, Pamelor, Sinequan

MAOIs: Nardil, Parnate

SSRIs: Prozac, Paxil, Zoloft, Celexa, Luvox, Lexapro

Other: Effexor, Remeron, Cymbalta

Good News:
- Generally effective
- Not addictive like benzodiazepines
- Tricyclics are particularly inexpensive

Bad News:

- Can take weeks to months to work (usually two to six weeks)
- Anxiety can become worse before it gets better
- Temporary side effects: headache, sweating, dizziness, insomnia
- Temporary and sometimes ongoing sexual side effects, e.g., loss of sex drive or inability to have erection or climax
- Tricyclics and MAOIs can be unsafe, if not lethal, due to numerous side effects

II: Benzodiazepines

Examples: Valium, Librium, Xanax, Ativan, Klonopin

Good news:

- They offer immediate relief, usually within hours
- Excellent sleep aides, especially if used to initiate sleep

Bad news:

- Can have sedative effect; if the dose is too high, intoxication can result
- They are more likely to produce a psychological dependence and sometimes a physiological dependence—especially if you have a history of alcohol dependence
- Certain types of benzodiazepines (those with a short half-life) can produce withdrawal and possibly seizure if stopped abruptly after several months; although this is a rare event, it can be life-threatening

III. BuSpar

Good News:

- Doesn't lead to dependency
- Sometimes used successfully to restore sexual functioning impaired by antidepressants

Bad News:

- Effective with fewer individuals than the benzodiazepines
- Takes three to four weeks to work

IV. Anticonvulsants

Example: Neurontin

Good News:
- Seems to be effective at calming anxiety
- Improves sleep

Bad News:
- Side effects include sleepiness, dizziness, and "brainfog"

V. Beta-Blockers

Example: Inderal

Good News:
- Reduces physical "fight-or-flight" symptoms, such as increased heart rate, sweating, shaking, and shortness of breath
- Helpful in calming performance anxiety before public speaking or test-taking

Bad News:
- Very short-term effect
- Physical effects, such as slowed heart rate, can be problematic

VI. Antihistamines

Examples: Benadryl, Vistaril

Good News:
- Calming, sedating effect
- Non-addictive, so there is less concern about potential for dependence

Bad News:
- Not as effective as other medications for anxiety
- Side effects include drowsiness, dry mouth, constipation, and urinary retention

I've heard that benzodiazepines have many side effects. What are they? Is BuSpar a good alternative?

Benzodiazepines can promote calmness by increasing the level of GABA in your brain. However, they can also produce sedation and grogginess, lack of balance, and impaired memory. Other risks of use include:

- Excess muscle relaxation that can compromise breathing in people who have lung disease (respiratory suppression)
- Accident proneness, especially if combined with alcohol
- Psychological and/or physiological dependence for some individuals
- Recovering alcoholics who use benzodiazepines may lose control of their abstinence behavior.

Lowering the dose of the medicine can reduce some of these side effects.

Whereas benzodiazepines work on GABA, Buspirone, or BuSpar, is known as a partial 5HT agonist—this means it helps to increase the level of serotonin in your brain. It can be a good alternative for those concerned about the addictive potential of the benzodiazepines. BuSpar has the following advantages: it does not interact with alcohol to promote intoxication, lead to dependency, or cause impairment of mechanical performance like driving a car. In contrast to the quick action of the benzodiazepines, however, BuSpar can take several weeks to work, gradually reducing anxiety over time. BuSpar's side effects include nausea, headache, nervousness, insomnia, dizziness, and lightheadedness.

Of the medications currently available for anxiety, which are having the most success?

The most popular medications for the treatment of anxiety are the newest class of antidepressants, the SSRIs—Prozac, Zoloft, Paxil, Lexapro, and Celexa. Some of the non-SSRI antidepressants (for instance, Effexor) are also promising.

Since the 1960s, the stand-by medicines for anxiety have been the benzodiazepines, known by names such as Valium, Librium, Ativan, Xanax, and Klonopin. They are quite effective and work quickly. They can also be sedating and are often used to help with insomnia. The biggest disadvantage of these drugs is that some people can become psychologically and/or physiologically dependent on them. Sometimes, a person may get a "buzz" from one of these drugs and subsequently abuse it like alcohol or other intoxicating substances. If a person becomes physiologically addicted, sudden withdrawal has been known to lead to seizures and even death. A subtler side effect of these drugs is a very slight loss of memory.

Unlike the benzodiazepines, the SSRIs were designed to treat depression. However, abundant research and clinical practice have shown that they are also effective in combating many forms of anxiety. Today, SSRIs are considered the first-line medication treatment for anxiety. Whereas SSRIs take longer to work—sometimes several weeks—they don't lead to marked physiological dependence. Sudden discontinuation of some SSRIs is associated with uncomfortable withdrawal-like symptoms, although rarely associated with seizures or death. Additionally, SSRIs do not produce an intoxicated feeling, and they generally do not impair memory. Unfortunately, SSRIs are usually more expensive because most of the patents on these drugs have not expired. Older antidepressants, such as tricyclics and monoamine oxidase inhibitors, can be effective in treating anxiety and are often less expensive. The downside is that they are loaded with side effects and are less safe than the SSRIs.

What are the side effects of the tricyclic and MAOI antidepressants?

The side effects of the tricyclics are many, and some can be danger-ous. Initially, patients can experience dry mouth, constipation, urinary retention, orthostatic hypotension (sudden lowering of blood pressure upon standing up), blurred vision, tachycardia (increased heart rate), and rarely, cardiac arrhythmias (with high doses). In the long-run, it is common to see weight gain and sexual dysfunction. If one overdoses on these medicines, the result can be fatal.

Common side effects of the MAOIs include orthostatic hypoten-sion, headache, insomnia, weight gain, sexual dysfunction, peripheral edema (swelling), and afternoon sleepiness. If taken with certain for-bidden foods or beverages (ones that contain tyramine—including aged cheeses, smoked meats, and certain wines), blood pressure can escalate and lead to a hypertensive crisis and possible stroke. Individuals taking these medications must be on a restricted diet.

Sedation is common in these medications, and some of them help individuals sleep better. Unfortunately, anxiety symptoms may worsen on initiation of these medicines—and any other antidepres-sants. The initial doses are best started low and slowly increased to therapeutic doses to keep this side effect to a minimum. Some doc-tors will start patients on a combination of an antidepressant and a benzodiazepine. It takes several weeks for the antidepressant to have an antianxiety or antidepressant effect. The benzodiazepines work quickly and can help the patient until the antidepressant kicks in.

What are the side effects of the SSRI and SSRI-like antidepressants?

Initial side effects of SSRIs often include mild nausea, loose bowel movements, anxiety, headache, and sweating. They usually disappear after a few weeks. Individuals taking SSRIs for an extended period of time may complain of weight gain. With some of the SSRIs, it is not uncommon to have sexual dysfunction. This is a later side effect and may remain until the medication is discontinued. For men, it may mean low desire, difficulty achieving an erection, trouble ejaculating, or delayed ejaculation (which is why this class of drugs is used in treating premature ejaculation). For women, it may mean low desire, trouble lubricating, or difficulty having an orgasm. Some people complain of sedation with these medications. It is usually helpful to have them taken before bedtime if that occurs. An additional side effect of the SSRIs is that patients occasionally report very vivid dreams.

The most harmful side effect, though rare, is serotonin syndrome. It is most likely to occur if two or more serotonergic medications are used simultaneously. Although there are isolated examples of this syndrome with one SSRI, the most important combination of drugs to avoid is that of an SSRI and an MAOI. Serotonin syndrome starts out with lethargy, restlessness, confusion, flushing, sweating, tremor, and sudden jerking of the feet. It can progress to increased temperature, generalized muscle rigidity, kidney failure, and even death.

In general, however, the side effects of the SSRIs are easier to tolerate than those of the tricyclics or the MAOIs. SSRIs are also much safer to use and are less dangerous if someone overdoses on them.

Side effects of Effexor (venlafaxine) are similar to the SSRIs except occasionally, when a modest rise in blood pressure occurs. Remeron (mirtazepine) can induce sleep when used at lower doses, and also has a high likelihood of causing weight gain.

My doctor mentioned that drugs like Neurontin and Inderal are being used to treat anxiety. Are they safe? What are the side effects?

Neurontin (gabapentin), an anticonvulsant, is a relatively safe medication, and is popular with psychiatrists and patients because it doesn't require monitoring of blood levels, as do other anticonvulsants. The side effects of Neurontin include dizziness, blurred vision (diplopia), lack of balance (ataxia), sleepiness (somnolence), and fatigue. Patients are advised not to drive or operate complex machinery until they have enough experience with the drug to know that it will not affect their performance. Another warning with Neurontin is that very rarely, the sudden discontinuation of the medication could result in a seizure.

Inderal (propranolol), a beta-blocker, is usually safe to use, but requires medical supervision. As with any prescription drug, don't be tempted to use a pill offered by a friend or family member. Inderal is not safe for individuals with asthma or severe breathing problems, as it can worsen these conditions. Side effects of Inderal include slowing of heart rate (bradycardia), lowered blood pressure (hypotension), cardiac arrhythmia, congestive heart failure for those at risk, depression, fatigue, lightheadedness, nausea, vomiting, diarrhea, and cramping.

What new drugs are being studied for anxiety? How are researchers hoping to improve on current medications?

Researchers are trying to develop new drugs that combine the benefits of benzodiazepines (the fast action) with the benefits of the SSRIs (effectiveness with fewer side effects). Parallel to new brain research, drug studies are focusing on the receptor for the body's natural tranquilizer, GABA. While GABA's anxiety-inhibiting effect was the basis for the development of the benzodiazepines, new research is zooming in on the receiving center for GABA and identifying specialized subunits—sort of like different lines coming into a phone center. Whereas benzodiazepines, like Valium, work across all the subunits at once, new drugs aim to specify which combinations of subunits to activate. Several pharmaceutical research labs are currently trying to produce fast-acting anxiety medications that don't include the addictive potential, sedation, memory impairment, or lack of coordination associated with existing benzodiazepines.

What are the long-term side effects of medications advertised on television, like Zoloft and Paxil?

The long-term side effects of the SSRIs, like Zoloft and Paxil, are fairly benign for adults. In general, they may cause weight gain or interference with sexual function. In some cases, sleep disturbance may be a long-term effect. A few people also complain of losing their normal range of emotions and may describe their feelings as numb.

When SSRIs are combined with a number of other drugs, other concerns may arise, such as the increased risk of liver toxicity. This risk is most likely in a small subset of the population (about 5 to 10%) who has a genetic predisposition to poor metabolism of medications.

Women who want to become pregnant or breast-feed should consult with their physicians or pharmacists regarding taking any of these medications. There can be adverse consequencess on the developing fetus or the nursing child. The long-term effects of these drugs on children and adolescents are less well-known.

Of course, if a person develops other illnesses and/or takes other kinds of medicines, the side effect profile might change considerably. Again, it is wise to consult with your physician.

What should I be aware of if I decide to take medication for my anxiety?

When considering medication for the treatment of anxiety, here are some suggestions.

- When you tell your doctor about medications you are already using, make sure to include any over-the-counter drugs or alternative medicines, such as herbal supplements. Although we may think of these medicines as harmless, some can cause serious problems when combined with prescription medication.
- If the prescribing doctor is new to you, make sure he or she is aware of any medical conditions—such as cardiac problems, high blood pressure, low blood pressure, pregnancy, nursing, and addictions—that could complicate your treatment.
- Ask your doctor how the medication works and what to expect when you take the drug. What are the intended effects, and what are the side effects?
- Find out what side effects signal the need for medical attention.
- As much as we like to think of doctors as magicians, they rely on you to let them know what works and doesn't work. Sometimes, the initial prescription and dosage are just right for you. Other times, you need to work with your doctor to figure out the right dosage of the right medication. The process can sometimes feel discouraging, but stick with it. The rewards are worth it.

- Ask your doctor up front how you would go about stopping the medication if it would need to be discontinued. *It can be dangerous to stop certain medicines abruptly*, and these need to be tapered off slowly under your doctor's supervision.
- Follow your doctor's directions for when and how to take your medications, and expect the best.

If I stop taking an antianxiety medicine, will I get anxious again?

If nothing else has changed, you may become anxious again. The reason is that most anxiety disorders are chronic and wax and wane over time. You may feel better with the anxiety medication, and then assume you are ready to stop your treatment, only to find that the anxiety returns. Here are some important exceptions:

1. Sometimes, our anxiety is associated with a life crisis—e.g., disaster, loss of a loved one—and will resolve on its own whether or not we use medication to aid our adjustment. In these cases, stopping the medications after a few months may not lead to increased anxiety.
2. If you have completed a successful course of psychotherapy while on medication, you may not experience a return of symptoms when you stop the medicine. Many factors contribute to the production of anxiety symptoms, including past experiences, your defenses, avoidance behaviors, and the way you think. These factors can often be identified in psychotherapy and remedied accordingly.

If you decide to stop your medications, talk to your physician about how to do so. As noted earlier, some anxiety medications are dangerous to stop abruptly.

To control my anxiety, will I have to take medications all my life?

How long you need to take medication depends on many factors including the type of anxiety disorder, the presence of other disorders or illness, and whether you've gone through a course of psychotherapy. It also seems that the earlier the disorder started (e.g., age 10 or 11), the more chronic and tenacious the illness may be, and the more likely medications might be needed long-term. Another factor that may suggest a more persistent illness requiring medication is the presence of serious psychiatric disorders among many close relatives.

Fortunately, as a result of comprehensive research studies, physicians have guidelines that recommend the length of medication usage for particular problems with anxiety. The good news is that you do not need to make this call on your own. Let your prescribing doctor and your therapist, if you have one, help you determine if and when you are ready to discontinue your medications. Gradually decreasing the dosage often makes it easier to wean off a medication, and sometimes, this is the only safe way to go.

Further, there are psychotherapies that have been shown to treat anxiety disorders effectively. In fact, certain types of therapy have proven superior to medication in the long-term treatment of some anxiety disorders (e.g., cognitive-behavioral therapy for panic disorder). This may be because the skills learned in cognitive-behavioral therapy help an individual cope with panic on his own. Moreover, these skills are with him for the long-term and not discontinued like medications.

In pursuing psychotherapy for the treatment of anxiety, the individual should be prepared to assume responsibility for tackling the problem. Neither a prescribing physician nor a psychotherapist offers a magic remedy to remove anxiety. Ultimately, the patient must face her fears and demonstrate to herself that she will survive in spite of them.

It is not unusual to stop medicines and go many years without a return of anxiety symptoms, only to have them appear again. Do not despair. This often stems from severe stress or the development of another mental or physical disorder. With proper evaluation and treatment—a course of medications and/or psychotherapy—it is common to see anxiety symptoms diminish again.

Are there any medications that are okay for someone over 70 to take for anxiety?

The SSRI antidepressants are effective for treating many anxiety disorders and are generally safe for older adults. However, they can have some uncomfortable side effects. For example, taking Paxil, which has more anticholinergic properties, may result in mild interference with memory. In general, the main drawbacks of SSRIs are that they can induce more anxiety at first, and they take a fairly long time to work (anywhere from 2 to 10 weeks). Doses for older individuals may also need to be lower than usual starting amounts.

The benzodiazepines are commonly used to treat anxiety, but they can create problems for older individuals. These medications may interfere with memory when memory may already be failing. If taken before bedtime, they may make it difficult to wake up and use the bathroom at night. Benzodiazepines may increase the risk of stumbling and falling. If there are any breathing problems, these medications may over-sedate the breathing muscles and cause problems with more shortness of breath. Increased anxiety may follow when people feel like they can't breathe adequately.

Chapter 5

WORRIES ABOUT WORRY

- Why do I worry?
- As long as I can get reassurance from one of my family members about my worries, I feel better. Do I still need to seek treatment for my worrying?
- I always worry about my health. People tell me I am a hypochondriac. What can I do about this?
- What is generalized anxiety disorder, and how do I know if I have it?
- My mother worried all the time, and I tend to worry a lot, too. Does that mean I'm going to be a worrier for the rest of my life like she is?
- Is it normal to worry about what people think of me?
- Every once in a while, I have a thought about doing something "out there" like throwing something at my neighbor or telling off my boss. Does this mean I'm crazy?
- My son is a police officer. Every day, I worry I will get a call that he is dead or hurt. How can I live a healthy life with this constant worry?
- A part of me thinks my partner is cheating on me. I worry about it all the time. What can I do to resolve this anxiety?
- What can help with worrying so much about the way I look?
- I feel guilty about being so anxious, and I worry about how this will affect my children. What should I do?
- Does being a perfectionist affect anxiety?
- Are procrastination and anxiety related?
- Is it possible to learn to procrastinate less?
- Can anxiety make me angry?
- I'm constantly worrying about my son's school performance. He never seems to study as much as I think he should. What can I do to make him work harder?
- I overeat when I'm anxious. What can I do about this problem?

Why do I worry?

Many factors contribute to worrying, including your biology, past experiences, the current environment, and your thought processes. To understand worry, it can be very helpful to explore self-talk (what a person is saying to himself moment-to-moment and deeper beliefs that may be creating or fueling anxiety). Worrying is usually associated with "what if?" thinking in which a person consistently overestimates threats or danger and underestimates his ability to cope. Many individuals also have superstitious or magical beliefs about worrying. For example, some people hold the false assumption that worry protects them or loved ones. Here are some of the thoughts individuals may use to justify worry:

- If I stay worried about Joe, he will feel better knowing that I am thinking about him. People like to know you have them in your thoughts and prayers. It's the proper thing to do.
- Worrying about others shows I'm a caring and unselfish person.
- Others may be harmed if I don't keep them in my thoughts. I have to worry to protect them and me.
- God will see what I sacrifice to make others happy and reward me.

As indicated above, some people view worry as a way of producing results in the world, when in reality, action is required to produce results. Repeated reassurance-seeking as well as avoidance behaviors may also maintain excessive worrying. These strategies offer short-term gain at the cost of long-term pain. When a person constantly relies on others to make her feel better, the worrisome thoughts might subside temporarily, but they tend to be strengthened over the long-run. This also happens with the use of avoidance behaviors. Repeatedly calling your daughter at college to make sure she is safe or not going to work because you are afraid you made a mistake on a report are examples of behaviors that actually give worry more power over you. Resisting making the call to your daughter and going into work despite the mistake are ways that you show yourself "It wasn't as bad as I thought" and "I can handle this even if it is uncomfortable." These thinking and behavior changes are essential for chipping away at your worry!

There is no simple answer to the question "Why do I worry?" but do keep in mind that worry is a habitual way of negative thinking that can be improved.

As long as I can get reassurance from one of my family members about my worries, I feel better. Do I still need to seek treatment for my worrying?

This depends on the extent and severity of your worrying. If the following statements are true for you, then it might be a good idea to seek professional treatment:

- My worry feels out of control.
- I feel like I can't stop worrying.
- My worry causes me a great deal of distress.
- My worry causes problems with my family, social, work, and recreational activities.

Reassurance from a family member or even a close friend can be helpful in the moment, but over time your problems with worry are likely to persist. Reassurance-seeking is recognized by professionals as a "safety behavior," or a short-term coping mechanism. Let's say I worry that my husband has been in a car accident, even though there is no evidence for that. I ask my sister, "Is he okay? Did anything happen to him?" and she tells me, "He's fine...everything is fine." I might feel better at the time, but I haven't learned anything as far as how to look at my negative thinking in a more realistic manner. What I've learned is that every time I worry about my husband, I can ask my sister about it to feel better. To really begin to make a dent in your worrying, you don't want to have to depend on anyone's reassurance. You want to learn to be your own rational coach or reassurer.

I always worry about my health. People tell me I am a hypochondriac. What can I do about this?

Hypochondriasis is a disorder where someone fears developing, or believes she already has, a dreaded disease and repeatedly seeks medical attention. She is preoccupied with her health and commonly misinterprets harmless bodily sensations as indicative of serious illness. In her mind, something is really wrong with her, and the doctors keep missing the problem. She continues to pursue appointments with physicians to increase the chance of "getting to the bottom of the matter," and she hates to be called a hypochondriac. Despite the accumulated evidence suggesting no dangerous illness, the hypochondriac doesn't consider her beliefs to be irrational or unreasonable. Most individuals with hypochondriasis are so focused on the idea of having a severe medical problem that the other matters in their life take a back seat. The vocational, romantic, family, and recreational aspects of their lives are often in shambles, and they don't recognize it.

Whereas patients frequently visit their doctors to feel better, hypochondriasis actually persists because of repeated medical examination and reassurance. People seek temporary relief strategies that ultimately keep them from disconfirming their incorrect, unhelpful, exaggerated illness beliefs. Getting better means learning alternative explanations for bodily sensations and practicing believing more accurate, realistic explanations related to one's health. Additionally, it is essential to decrease the "safety behaviors" (e.g., looking on the internet, reading medical texts, taking blood pressure and temperature) and reassurance-seeking (e.g., visiting a doctor, calling the doctor's nurse) that actually maintain the excessive worry over time.

What is generalized anxiety disorder, and how do I know if I have it?

Generalized anxiety disorder (GAD) is, as the name implies, anxiety or worry that comes up often and in a variety of situations, and is out of proportion with the realities of these situations. People with generalized anxiety disorder worry about their health, family members' health, their own academic and work performance, others' academic and work performance, finances, the neighborhood, church, terrorism, etc. Sufferers of GAD may feel as if they bounce around from one worry to the next and may be uncomfortable if they're not worrying about something. GAD is diagnosed when:

- Excessive worry and anxiety about a number of life circumstances occur more days than not for at least six months
- The worry is hard for the person to control
- Three or more of the following symptoms accompany the anxiety:
  - Restlessness or feeling "keyed up" or on edge
  - Getting tired easily
  - Difficulty concentrating or mind going blank
  - Irritability
  - Muscle tension
  - Sleep disturbance
- The focus of the anxiety and worry is not confined to another anxiety disorder

- The anxiety and accompanying symptoms cause significant distress or limit social, occupational or other important areas of functioning

If you meet most or all of these criteria, you should consider contacting a mental health professional for proper evaluation and treatment.

My mother worried all the time, and I tend to worry a lot, too. Does that mean I'm going to be a worrier for the rest of my life like she is?

Worry is based on self-talk. Often when people worry excessively, they overestimate danger in the world and underestimate their ability to cope. Just because your mother worried a lot does not automatically mean you are going to be a worrier for the rest of your life. Worrying can become a habit, but all habits can be changed with hard work. When you start to worry, instead of letting your mind toss around "what if this and what if that?" it is a good idea to flesh out what is most likely to happen. Focus on probabilities (likelihoods) rather than remote possibilities. Also, ask yourself, "What's the worst- case scenario and how would I deal with it?"

Perhaps your mother was afraid to drive and never drove her car. This is a behavior that can change if a person is willing to question some of her negative assumptions. Your mother might have said to herself, "I can't drive—I'll crash...What if I totaled the car?...What if I hurt somebody else?...What if I became paralyzed?" If that is what she believed, it makes sense she would feel anxious about driving and probably avoid it. However, it might have been good for her to question, "Why can't I learn to drive a car?" and "Even though car accidents happen, what makes it certain I'm going to have a car accident if I try to drive?" Worrisome thoughts can be identified, evaluated and disputed, but it takes consistent effort. Remember also that life contains hassles, problems, and nuisances, so an absence of any distressing emotion is not going to be realistic. However, if you notice yourself worrying excessively, you might decide you prefer appropriate concern to excessive worry. The difference between worries and concerns depends on your thinking!

Is it normal to worry about what people think of me?

In the way that the outdoor temperature is reflected in degrees on a thermometer, it's helpful to think of worry as occurring at different levels instead of as an all-or-nothing emotion. It is completely normal to be concerned about what people think of us. We live in a social world, and interaction with other people is vital. Naturally, we want others to think well of us. Getting along well with others feels good and often helps us reach our social and professional goals.

Yet, focusing on the views of others can make us overly cautious and anxious. Here are some signs that your focus is excessive or unhealthy:

- You don't feel good about yourself, and are **projecting** your negative feelings. For example, you imagine your boss is unhappy with your work rather than admitting that you aren't happy with your performance.
- You may be engaging in a thinking mistake known as **mind-reading**—assuming that you know what a person is thinking about you when you actually have no evidence for your conclusion.
- You tell yourself that it's *terrible* if someone doesn't like you, when maybe it's just inconvenient. Another person's view of you is not a measure of your worth unless you allow it to be.

To shift these tendencies, give yourself credit for your strengths and practice learning to accept your mistakes—we all make them! And keep in mind that most people are more focused on their own priorities and interests than on thinking about you. To illustrate this point, try writing down all the topics that others could be considering or discussing, *besides you!* You'll find that this list is endless!

Every once in a while, I have a thought about doing something "out there" like throwing something at my neighbor or telling off my boss. Does this mean I'm crazy?

Studies have shown that 85-90% of ordinary people experience intrusive thoughts or mental images that they consider distressing or disruptive. Just because negative thoughts come into your mind, that does not make you crazy or abnormal. What distinguishes normal intrusive thoughts from psychotic or delusional thoughts is that the latter involve a break with reality. For example, a psychotic person may believe that the thought originates from a higher authority, such as Jesus Christ, and may even hear the thought as an actual voice (auditory hallucination). The person may then feel that he has no choice but to obey.

It is normal to have thoughts about things you would not actually do. You will become needlessly anxious if you attach great significance to the negative thoughts. If you have a negative and impulsive thought like "I'm going to embarrass my boss in front of everybody," and then you say to yourself, "Because I have this thought, I'm a horrible person" or "That was terrible of me," you are going to be a lot more bothered than if you can say to yourself, "It's just a thought, and I know I wouldn't act on it."

My son is a police officer. Every day, I worry I will get a call that he is dead or hurt. How can I live a healthy life with this constant worry?

Anybody with a loved one working in dangerous conditions such as police work or the military would feel concern. The degree of concern, however, depends on how you think about this situation. Keep in mind that it is not really your loved one's work that causes your constant worry. Rather, it is what you tell yourself about his work. If you are saying to yourself, "Today will be the day I get the call that he's been killed," here's what might be going on in your head:

1. You are telling yourself something is going to happen at a certain point in time. This type of thinking (self-talk) is called **fortune-telling**.
2. You are also jumping to the worst conclusion about what could happen. This is called **catastrophizing**.
3. At the same time that you are overestimating the danger and threat of the situation, you are underestimating your own or a loved one's ability to cope.

One of the best ways to deal with constant worrying is to learn to challenge negative predictions and develop more realistic views of situations and coping resources. For example, you might remind yourself that your loved one is doing the job she wants to do, that she is skilled, that she works with competent colleagues, and that she has handled difficult situations well in the past. Also note that there is a difference between possibilities (it could happen) and probabilities (it's likely to happen). You could get a call that your loved one has been hurt or killed, but that's not the most likely outcome. We're better off when we resist turning small negative possibilities into probabilities. Life has no guarantees, but learning and practicing more realistic self-talk can help you better tolerate uncertainties.

Further, it's important to realize that we can't see into the future—you are not God, and no one has a crystal ball. The truest statement we can make about the future is that we don't know what it holds. Therefore, it is best to try to live in the moment. Sometimes our focus on someone else's well-being can be a way of avoiding attending to our own lives. Start focusing on spending your time in ways that feel meaningful and productive—maybe through becoming more engaged in your own work, getting together with friends, or starting something new, like a hobby or volunteering.

Finally, we sometimes worry because we believe that our worry magically protects others. Or, we believe the person we're concerned about not only wants us to be concerned about them, but to worry about them. We think that he will feel better in a dangerous situation if he knows we are constantly worrying about him. These ideas overestimate the effects of worry for any benefit. In fact, these beliefs are akin to believing in magic. We have no evidence that worry benefits anyone, but we do know that it causes the worrier harm. If you want to help your loved one, focus on what you *can* control. Send a care package, help out, express your love. It's generally better to control those aspects of your life you can *actually* control than those aspects of your life where the only control is through magic.

A part of me thinks my partner is cheating on me. I worry about it all the time. What can I do to resolve this anxiety?

This is where you have to ask yourself if your worry is based on reason and fact or on imagination and fantasy. If you have a basis for your worry, you may allow the feelings to eat away at you rather than face the truth. The most direct way to discover the truth is to look your partner in the eyes and ask. To find out if you're imagining things, ask yourself the following questions, and be honest with yourself:

- Do I have any evidence?
- Is my evidence substantial?
- If I ask my partner if he is having an affair, and he says "no", will I believe him?
- Is there any way he could convince me that he isn't having an affair?
- If I hire a private detective to determine if there is an affair and the detective says "no," would I believe her?

If your answers show that even though you don't have any evidence, your partner would deny it, and a detective would find no evidence, you would still worry—then your worry may be excessive. In this case, your worry is not based on fact or reason. Some people in this situation can be reassured but only temporarily. Treatment is often necessary because this kind of worry can easily take over your life and destroy your relationship.

If you get therapy, you may discover that there is indeed something you wish were different about your spouse or your relationship. It may be something you can speak with him about. He may or may not be willing to change, but you can have the satisfaction of knowing the truth about your own worries and knowing you took measures to address them.

What can help with worrying so much about the way I look?

We live in a society that emphasizes appearance as the means to success and happiness. Given the media's bombardment of perfect-looking images, it is difficult not to compare yourself to television and film figures and magazine covers and come up short. Despite societal influences, however, the way a person looks doesn't produce worry or distress—rather, a person's thoughts about her appearance are the culprit. What are you saying to yourself about how you look? If you tell yourself that you look terrible, it's not surprising that you would feel anxious and depressed. But what's the evidence that you look terrible even if you don't resemble a magazine cover? Where is it getting you to think, "I look terrible"? Resisting unhelpful societal demands to look a certain way and learning to separate your appearance from your worth as a person are very important goals in improving emotional well-being. Growing up, perhaps you learned that self-value was based on having a particular body image. Now is an excellent time to question this old assumption. Inevitably, people get older, and physical changes will occur. If you awfulize these changes and condemn yourself for them, you will feel much worse than if you learn to tolerate the physical differences and accept yourself anyway. Again, using effective, forceful self-talk is key.

Anxiety-Generating Self-Talk
- I must look perfect or I'm no good.
- Everyone can see this flaw—how terrible!
- I can't stand this flaw.

- I can't be happy until I lose weight.
- I hate my body!

Anxiety-Reducing Self-Talk
- Nobody looks perfect all the time, and appearance is not the gauge of my worth.
- People are far more focused on themselves than on anything about me. I look fine!
- Even if I don't like this particular body part, I certainly can stand it. There's much more to me than this one feature.
- If I'd like to lose weight, I can work on this goal, but it doesn't determine my level of happiness. Moreover, putting appearance-based demands on myself just makes me more anxious and interferes with reaching my goals.
- My body can do an amazing number of activities! Why condemn it because it doesn't look like a movie star's body? I would never judge anyone else as harshly as I'm judging myself.

It is important to note that some people are so focused on per-ceived physical flaws that it becomes consuming. **Body dysmorphic disorder** is an increasingly recognized mental disorder in which a per-son is preoccupied with an imagined or slight deficit in appearance (e.g., "crooked" nose, facial lines, acne scars, thinning hair). Other peo-ple might not even notice what the individual is concerned about, but the BDD sufferer believes the flaw is repulsive. As a result, she may engage in compulsive mirror-checking or mirror-avoidance, over-grooming, skin-picking, cosmetic procedures, or reassurance-seeking. In addition to avoiding school, work, and social activities, people with body dysmorphic disorder tend to report high levels of distress and suicidal ideation and attempts. Other appearance-related, highly-distressing clinical conditions include eating disorders, which are prevalent in women and increasing in men. Both cognitive-behavioral therapy and medications (SSRIs) can be effective in treating eating disorders and body dysmorphic disorder. Early diagnosis and intervention are vital in offsetting the harmful effects of these conditions.

I feel guilty about being so anxious, and I worry about how this will affect my children. What should I do?

To feel guilty, a person is usually thinking something along the following lines—"I did something wrong and because of this, I'm a bad person." One of the best things you can do for yourself is to challenge your guilt-producing self-talk. You are already struggling with an anxiety problem that you didn't ask for or desire—that's enough to deal with! When you add on guilt, now you have two problems—your anxiety and your guilt. Focusing on the guilt is going to leave you with fewer resources to devote to improving your anxiety.

Once you actively resist focusing on how bad you are for feeling anxious (which is not true!), it is a good idea to be concerned about how your anxiety might affect your children. Although you want your children to be aware of safety issues and true dangers in the world, it's important for them to grow up believing the world is a relatively safe, predictable place and that they can cope with difficulties. These types of ideas promote healthier adjustment than beliefs that the world is dangerous and they can't cope. Notice the type of messages you're communicating to your children. As you provide more calming messages, you may also be comforted. Likewise, when you talk to yourself with more trust and less condemnation, your children will pick up on your new attitude.

Acknowledging that you struggle with anxiety and seeking assistance also provide good modeling to children—which may encourage them to feel better about getting help when they need it.

Does being a perfectionist affect anxiety?

Perfectionistic tendencies can contribute to feeling anxious. If you believe that everything you do must be perfect, you will feel anxious because nobody can do everything perfectly. People can strive for excellence, but when we demand perfection, we set ourselves up for problems. Perfectionistic people tend to think in black-and-white terms and believe there is absolutely one right way to do things. It is hard for them to see gray areas or realize 85% or 90% effort will produce very satisfactory results most of the time.

The sad thing about perfectionism is that it keeps you in a deficit situation. Rather than starting with a clean slate and seeing everything you accomplish as gains, you start at a 100% expectation, and all you see is what puts you below this. When you notice the deficit, you become anxious because you are not meeting your unrealistic expectation.

A simple way to begin correcting this situation is to start every day with a clean slate. Notice what you add just by being who you are ("I make people laugh"), notice the many things you do that you may not usually give yourself credit for ("I fed my kids, watered the plants, walked the dog"), and especially, notice how you're learning and growing. The irony here is that it is often through our *mistakes* that we learn and grow!

There is nothing wrong with striving for excellence. In fact, people who have visions of great things tend to achieve great things. Further, individuals who give themselves credit for what they've accomplished tend to realize their goals more than people who tear themselves down for what they haven't perfected.

Are procrastination and anxiety related?

Procrastination and anxiety are related in several ways. Initially, a person who feels anxious about a task may delay doing it. The reasons for this delay may include thoughts like "It's too hard...I'll never do it well enough...They won't think it's good enough." If you have these thoughts, then of course you are going to feel anxious, and it is not that surprising that you delay, fearing what needs to be done. Once you've procrastinated for a while and a deadline approaches, you may find yourself feeling even more anxious. Now, you are telling yourself "I've put this off for so long I'll never get it done...There's no way I'll finish in time...My boss will be mad at me because this report isn't complete." Again, it is these types of thoughts that make you anxious, not just the fact that the work hasn't been finished.

You can counter these negative thoughts with more realistic thoughts, such as, "I was assigned this project because I can do it." Second, get more information if you are not sure what is expected. Sometimes we make ourselves needlessly anxious because we imagine the task to be greater than it is. Finally, it can be very helpful to break the task into small pieces and focus on just the piece you are working on, rather than the final product.

Is it possible to learn to procrastinate less?

Procrastination is a habit that takes hard work to change, just like other habits. Ways to change procrastination behaviors include changing your thoughts and actually changing some of your actions. Thoughts that contribute to procrastination include "It's too hard...I'll do it later...I'll wait until I feel like it." Thoughts that help overcome procrastination include:

- "It's better for me to do it now than wait until later."
- "It's hard, but not too hard."
- "If I don't feel like it now, I'm probably not going to feel like it later, so it's better to go ahead and get it done."

This proactive type of thinking may promote concern and a little bit of irritation with the task you have to do, but the self-talk will keep your negative emotions at a level that allows you to get the work done.

Behaviors that can help with procrastination habits include taking action for five minutes. If there is something you desperately don't want to do, give yourself five minutes to work on the task. At the end of five minutes, you can decide, "Can I keep working on this or am I going to come back to this later?" It's interesting: once you get into something, it's often not as bad as you were thinking it was going to be before you started. With procrastination, it is very important not to wait for the motivation to do something—you'll just keep waiting. It is better to take action first, which can generate motivation and lead to more action. Keep in mind that it is worth it to put in the hard work to kick the procrastination habit. People who procrastinate find themselves feeling very anxious or stressed many times in their life.

Can anxiety make me angry?

People who struggle with anxiety often find that their tempers are shorter and that they feel more irritable. If you think about it, constantly worrying or constantly feeling like your body is revved up or on edge doesn't feel good. When you don't feel good internally, stressors that come up in your environment can have more of a negative impact on you. Obviously, anxiety and anger can be co-occurring conditions.

However, it is not really true to say that anxiety makes a person angry. What makes a person angry is his or her self-talk. Thoughts like "This shouldn't be happening to me," "I shouldn't have to put up with this," "They know I don't feel good," "They should treat me better," and "I've had enough, I can't take any more" are all going to increase your anxiety and anger. Further, when you are feeling anxious, there is a tendency to avoid normal activities and pleasurable activities. The more you avoid the kinds of things that give you enjoyment, the more likely problems with anger might be because you have no arena of comfort or outlet for distress.

I'm constantly worrying about my son's school performance. He never seems to study as much as I think he should. What can I do to make him work harder?

Remember, the only person's behavior that you can control or guarantee is your own. If you tell yourself, "My son doesn't study as much as he should…I need to make him work harder," that's basically putting your well-being in his hands. What may be truer is that you'd *like* your son to study more, work harder, and perform better in school, but there is no reason he absolutely must. If you realize this is a preference, knowing that you'd *like* it, but it doesn't absolutely *have* to happen, then you will feel appropriately concerned. If you are appropriately concerned, it's more levelheaded to set up a system of incentives and penalties for your son in regards to schoolwork. If, however, you tell yourself he *must* do better and he doesn't, your feeling will not be appropriate concern. Instead, your reaction will be anxiety. If you are anxious about this problem, you will have fewer resources to manage it. The bottom line here is that you will do better if you focus less on your *son's* behavior as a way to reduce your anxiety, and more on how *you* can think about this problem in a less upsetting way.

I overeat when I'm anxious. What can I do about this problem?

When we feel anxious, it's natural to want to feel better and get some comfort. However, it's probably no surprise to you that eating to feel better is a "short-term gain/long-term pain" option. You get some relief in the moment by tasting foods you enjoy, but over time, you develop a habit that's tough to break and gain more weight than you'd like.

To improve this problem, keep in mind that just feeling anxious isn't enough to get you to overeat. Many people can't eat at all when they experience anxiety. The important aspects to consider are what you're telling yourself and how you're responding when you're feeling anxious. If your self-talk is along the lines of "I can't stand this—I need something to make me feel better," then it makes sense that you might run to the refrigerator. However, this self-talk is likely untrue and certainly unhelpful. When you tell yourself that you can't stand something, you raise the stakes and generally increase the negative emotion you didn't want in the first place. Further, if you truly couldn't stand something, you'd die, which is not the case here. What's more accurate might be "I don't like how I feel right now, but I can stand it" and "I'd like something to help me feel better, but I don't need it to be food." When you can forcefully use more helpful, realistic self-talk, this strategy often keeps your emotional distress at a reasonable level, leaving you with more resources for managing your problems.

Whereas challenging unhelpful self-talk about anxiety and eating is extremely important, behavioral measures are also invaluable. Food is so readily available in such large quantities in our society that eating to feel better can become a mindless endeavor. At times, you may not even be aware of what you've eaten until after consuming far more calories than you wanted. So, having a clear idea of some helpful behaviors is important. Consider the following options.

- Keep a food log (see next page)—if you're not going to write it down, don't allow yourself to eat it!
- Don't bring home fattening foods or ones in which you're likely to overindulge.
- Have a list of enjoyable activities that don't include food. Post this list in your car, on the refrigerator, by your nightstand—anywhere that will catch your eye.
- Make a coping card or sign for the refrigerator or kitchen cabinets that alerts you to stop and think:

Bad feelings pass!
Is this stomach hunger or head hunger?
Do I really want food right now or am I just trying to feel less anxious?
How am I going to feel after I've eaten this?
How does eating this food now fit in with the nutritional goals I've set?

	Time of Day	Food and Amount	Setting and Situation	Head Hunger or Stomach Hunger?	Anxiety Level Before Eating (0–100)	Anxiety Level After Eating (0–100)
Sunday						
Monday						
Tuesday						
Wednesday						
Thursday						
Friday						
Saturday						

Chapter 6

UNDERSTANDING PANIC ATTACKS

- What is a panic attack?
- How does a panic attack happen?
- What's going on in my body when I have panic symptoms?
- What can I do to stop a panic attack?
- Can a panic attack hurt me?
- How do I know I'm not having a heart attack or a stroke when I panic?
- Is there a difference between anxiety attacks and panic attacks?
- Why do I feel like I'm losing control when I have a panic attack?
- Can I go crazy from a panic attack?
- Can stress cause a panic attack?
- I've heard that panic is like a vicious cycle. How does this work?
- What is a nervous breakdown? If my nerves act up, could I have one?
- I'm afraid I'm wearing my body out with my panic attacks. Can panic tear up my body?
- What is hyperventilation? Can it make me pass out?
- I feel like panic has taken over my life. How are other people limited by their panic attacks?
- My friends say they can't tell when I'm having a panic attack, but I know it's got to be so obvious. Can you help me understand this?
- I've heard that you can't have a panic attack if you're relaxed or if you're laughing. Why is that?
- I've had panic attacks during the day, but recently, I was jolted from sleep and found myself in the middle of a panic attack. Is this normal?
- I try not to go outside too much in the summer because I'm afraid I'll have a panic attack. Can heat make it more likely that I will panic?
- I've heard that panic attacks can lead to agoraphobia. Why? What is agoraphobia anyway?

What is a panic attack?

Each of us has probably felt "panicked" when faced with a crisis, meaning we got really scared or upset. A panic attack is different than just feeling panicky or nervous, however. A panic attack feels like a surge or a wave of fear coming over you. Typically, an attack lasts from a few minutes to half an hour, but the sensations can continue for longer periods. During a panic attack, you experience four or more of the following symptoms at the same time:

- Increased heart rate, pounding heart (palpitations)
- Sweating
- Trembling or shaking
- Shortness of breath or smothering sensations
- Feeling of choking
- Chest pain or discomfort
- Nausea or abdominal distress
- Dizziness or lightheadedness
- Feeling unreal or detached from yourself
- Fear of losing control or going crazy
- Fear of dying
- Numbness or tingling
- Chills or hot flushes

First, it is very important to rule out medical reasons for panic symptoms, such as cardiac, thyroid, or metabolic problems. Once your doctor has confirmed that there is no medical basis for your symptoms, it's a good bet that you're having a panic attack. As with other anxiety disorders, your body's alarm system is over-functioning. A panic attack is like one alarm setting off another until the whole building is screaming. Having a single symptom feels uncomfortable, but when several symptoms happen together all at once, the experience is quite frightening. In addition, the symptoms seem to come out of the blue. If you have suffered panic attacks, you may try to escape or avoid situations where you might panic again—work, the mall, restaurants, crowds, driving, being alone—and this can be debilitating. Although nobody likes to endure panic attacks, they are actually more common than you might think. During the past year, over 30% of individuals in the United States had some form of panic attack.

How does a panic attack happen?

Although it seems that a panic attack comes out of nowhere, it is more the case of one symptom building on another as we interpret the worst. Let's look at this example of a woman sitting at her desk at work:

Behavior: Notices her heart is beating a little faster

Thought: "Oh God, what's happening?"

Symptoms: Heart rate speeds up; breathing becomes shallower

Thoughts: "This is awful. Something must be wrong."

Behavior: Can't concentrate on work; looks for a way to escape; tries to gulp air

Symptoms: Heart races, shortness of breath intensifies; shaking and sweating develop

Thoughts: "I can't stand this. I've got to make it stop."

Symptoms: Pounding heart; pronounced shortness of breath; shaking and sweatiness continue; lightheadedness and nausea develop

➡

...and so on until she is engaged in a full-blown panic attack.

Once this woman has experienced a panic attack, she can develop a tremendous dread of having the symptoms recur. She often starts looking for and noticing any small changes in her bodily sensations. Becoming preoccupied with harmless body fluctuations can actually increase the chances of having more panic attacks. Negative thinking, shallow chest breathing, and avoiding previously enjoyable or productive activities out of fear of panic can also worsen and prolong problems with panic attacks.

What's going on in my body when I have panic symptoms?

Understanding the physical sensations that occur during a panic attack may be one of your best tools for coping with panic. Although it may be hard to believe, none of the sensations associated with panic is harmful in any way. In fact, these symptoms were originally intended to protect you from danger. To understand this point, it is helpful to think about our prehistoric ancestors. People living in cave times had one main objective—to stay alive. Survival basically meant being able to fight a predator or escape from one. To achieve this fight or flight goal, our ancestors' bodies needed to respond quickly and defensively against perceived threats. This response system has been passed on to us, and all the sensations that characterize a panic attack are actually part of what's known as our "fight-or-flight" ability. The following chart lists sensations that are common in panic attacks and how each symptom was linked to survival:

Symptom	Reason
Increased heart rate	An accelerated heart rate increases blood flow to the large muscles of the body (e.g., quadriceps, biceps), giving them more oxygen and helping them to prepare for fighting or running away.
Shortness of breath Chest pain Feeling of choking	Each of these symptoms is related to increased breathing. In the face of danger, our breathing accelerates to deliver more oxygen to the tissues involved in fighting or fleeing. (Think about times when you have run really fast.) One of the side effects is that the chest muscles are working really hard, which can result in chest pain or tightness.
Dizziness Lightheadedness Feeling unreal Feeling outside of yourself	These sensations are related to changes associated with the increased breathing rate during fighting or fleeing. As a result of overbreathing, slightly less oxygen reaches the brain. This change is not at all harmful, but it can lead to feeling lightheaded, faint, or confused.
Cold, clammy hands Numbness Tingling	Blood leaves the skin, fingers, and toes to keep a person from bleeding to death in the case of a severe cut or other wound. More blood is sent to the large muscle groups for fighting or getting away.

continued

Symptom	Reason
Sweating	This cools the body down. Sweating also makes the body more slippery, which hindered attackers' ability to grab and harm our cave ancestors.
Nausea or abdominal distress	Less activity is used for digestive processes—most of the body's energy and resources are being devoted to the large muscle groups for fighting or getting away from danger.
Trembling or shaking	Muscles can feel shaky because they are contracting to prepare for fighting or fleeing a threat.
Hot flushes	Preparing the body for fighting or running away uses a lot of energy, which results in feeling hot.

What can I do to stop a panic attack?

This may surprise you, but one of the best things you can do to decrease the severity of a panic attack is to remind yourself, "I don't have to absolutely stop this and I can stand these symptoms." The more you insist that you not have a panic attack or that the symptoms end immediately, the more anxious you actually make yourself. So, by focusing on stopping the attack, you can end up worsening the very symptoms you're trying to stop! Whether you are a new sufferer or an old sufferer of panic, keep in mind that panic attacks are not going to kill you, they are not going to cause you to have a heart attack, and you can ride these symptoms out. Important coping statements include:

- "This is uncomfortable, but I've been through this before. I'll get through this one too."
- "I'm not dying. I *can* ride this out."
- "This is a nuisance, but not the end of the world."

Basically, you don't want to demand that a panic attack must not happen or must stop immediately. In fact, a very effective treatment called *interoceptive exposure* by teaching the sufferer to *bring on* panic attacks.

Can a panic attack hurt me?

Assuming medical causes have been ruled out and your doctor has indicated you are having panic attacks, you can be reassured that panic symptoms are *not dangerous*. When you are panicking you might notice your heart racing, your arms and legs shaking, increased sweatiness, dizziness, lightheadedness, or nausea. All of these symptoms are uncomfortable and can feel really scary; however, none of them will hurt you in any way. Remember, a panic attack occurs because your "fight-or-flight" system is being activated. The fight-or-flight system was designed to protect you. None of the symptoms of a panic attack are going to hurt you or kill you. If you've been suffering from panic for a while, another way to know you are not dying is to think back to how many panic attacks you've experienced. For some people, this number is in the hundreds. Obviously, if you've gone through hundreds of panic attacks and not died before, there is much evidence to suggest you won't die during this attack.

Further, keep in mind that a panic attack is always temporary. The chemicals that produce our emergency response will be broken down, so it is impossible for a panic attack to persist indefinitely. Whereas it is difficult to remember this in the midst of a panic attack, the understanding that panic sensations are temporary and not harmful is a huge part of coping with the problem. The more you learn to think realistically about panic symptoms and respond more helpfully to them, the better you'll feel.

How do I know I'm not having a heart attack or a stroke when I panic?

First, you want to make sure that you have undergone a comprehensive medical examination to rule out cardiovascular, respiratory, gastrointestinal, metabolic, endocrine/hormonal, neuromuscular, and vestibular reasons for your panic symptoms. Once you have been medically cleared, you can be assured that panic attacks do not trigger heart attacks or strokes. In particular, an electrocardiogram (EKG) will reveal noticeable electrical changes in the heart if there is cardiac disease; on the other hand, the EKG will only show a small increase in heart rate with panic attacks. Understanding the distinguishing factors between a heart attack or stroke and a panic attack is a valuable task for someone fighting panic—it is a good idea to question your medical doctor about these differences and write down what he or she says so you'll remember. The symptoms of a heart attack usually include increased chest pressure, chest pain, and breathlessness, with occasional palpitations and fainting. Heart attack symptoms typically worsen with physical exertion and lessen with rest. In contrast, panic symptoms can feel like they come out of the blue and can occur just as strongly at rest as during activity. Further, during a panic attack, blood pressure does not increase drastically enough or cut off the blood supply to the brain sufficiently to cause a stroke.

Is there a difference between anxiety attacks and panic attacks?

People tend to use the words "anxiety attacks" and "panic attacks" interchangeably. Whereas panic attacks have a clear definition in the diagnostic manual of mental disorders (DSM-IV), there is no distinct label for an anxiety attack. Keep in mind that panic attacks are acute and short-lived episodes of anxiety, where you are overcome by the physical experience of anxiety (e.g., heart racing, sweating, nausea), feel out of control, and worry you are dying or going crazy. Panic attacks can last a few minutes to about a half hour. Sometimes people use the term "anxiety attack" to describe this experience, but people also use it more broadly to describe the more anxious times in their lives. When a person is worrying intensely and feeling physically revved up over a period of hours or days, this is a different type of anxiety than panic—and possibly an indication of generalized anxiety disorder. Because treatment recommendations will be different depending on the type of anxiety disorder, it is important to get an accurate diagnosis from a trained professional.

Why do I feel like I'm losing control when I have a panic attack?

Panic symptoms can be very frightening, and people often think they can lead to a variety of bizarre behaviors (e.g., screaming out in a classroom, attacking someone else, running out of an important meeting, jumping out of a car, becoming paralyzed). However, feeling this anxious can trick us into believing things that are very unlikely.

Cognitive-behavioral therapy helps people to become more informed about panic and ways of dealing with it. One of the most important sayings in cognitive-behavioral therapy is "Feelings aren't facts." This is especially true in the midst of a panic attack. During a panic attack, the body has kicked in its fight-or-flight response via sympathetic nervous system activation. Your body is reacting as though real danger is present, although this is most likely a false alarm. Given that your body is preparing to cope with perceived threat, it is gearing up to get you out of harm's way. Even though it may feel exactly the opposite, *your protection is the body's foremost goal when panic symptoms are activated.* Therefore, it is important for you to keep in mind that you are not going to lose control. No mysterious force is going to overtake you during a panic attack. Although your mind might be insisting "I can't stand this!" *you really can stand something that you very much dislike.* The confusion, apprehension, and sense of unreality that go along with panic are certainly inconvenient and unpleasant, but these sensations do not render you incapable of functioning. During panic attacks, people can still talk in work meetings, drive a car, feed and change their babies, and perform other everyday activities. In fact, an important coping statement for dealing with panic is, "I can be anxious and still function adequately."

Can I go crazy from a panic attack?

No. Panic attacks do not make people go crazy, even though you might feel this way in the midst of a panic attack. We'll assume "going crazy" means losing touch with reality (e.g., having persistent hallucinations and/or delusions) and becoming unable to carry out the most basic life activities (e.g., personal hygiene). While panic symptoms are very uncomfortable and even exhausting at times, they do not have the ability to take away a person's sanity. *Panic attacks cannot render a person schizophrenic, psychotic, or delusional.* During panic, people may experience increased heart rate, shortness of breath, numbness, tingling, dizziness, muscle tension, chest tightness, nausea, sweating, and a sense of being unreal or outside of themselves to varying degrees. As noted previously, all of these symptoms were originally designed for protection, none of them is dangerous, and all of them are temporary. Clearly, symptoms that were designed to protect you are not going to make you go crazy. This is not to say that panic symptoms don't take a toll on your emotional well-being—obviously, people would rather not have to struggle with panic in their daily lives. However, actively and forcefully reminding yourself that panic symptoms are harmless and that they cannot make you crazy is one way of getting a better grip on the problem.

Can stress cause a panic attack?

Stress is one of the factors that can contribute to panic attacks. Here are some ways stress and other factors make panic attacks more likely:

- Being more stressed in your life can result in increased levels of adrenaline and other chemicals that might make you more likely to panic.
- During times of stress, people often hold their breath intermittently or do more shallow chest breathing—these behaviors often result in hyperventilation, which is associated with all sorts of bodily changes (e.g., shortness of breath, dizziness, numbness, tingling, chest pain).
- Being more focused on bodily changes can increase a person's susceptibility to panic.
- A person's biological predisposition to emotional disturbance is important to consider—if several family members have a history of experiencing panic attacks, then it's more likely that this individual might also struggle with panic.

When thinking about what produces panic attacks, keep in mind that there are biological, psychological, and stress-related contributors. A first panic attack can feel terrifying because a person has no idea what's happening or why. Ruling out medical reasons for panic-like symptoms is a very important first step. Once a person is medically cleared, however, it is important for him to understand that panic symptoms are annoying but not dangerous. Problems with panic are maintained and exacerbated by dreading and trying to avoid harmless physical symptoms.

I've heard that panic is like a vicious cycle. How does this work?

The following triangle shows how panic feelings, fearful thoughts, and avoidance behaviors are interrelated and perpetuate each other.

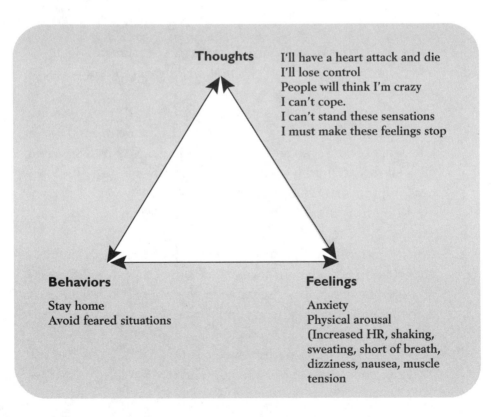

Thoughts

I'll have a heart attack and die
I'll lose control
People will think I'm crazy
I can't cope.
I can't stand these sensations
I must make these feelings stop

Behaviors

Stay home
Avoid feared situations

Feelings

Anxiety
Physical arousal
(Increased HR, shaking, sweating, short of breath, dizziness, nausea, muscle tension

What is a nervous breakdown? If my nerves act up, could I have one?

This term is a grab-bag phrase that applies to many mental illnesses. While people often refer to a mental health crisis as a "nervous breakdown," this is not a professional term, so it has no standard accepted meaning. It usually implies that someone has a mental illness of such severity that she can no longer cope, perform the activities of daily living, or think through ordinary problems. She may have lost her grip on reality and may need to be in a safe environment like a psychiatric hospital or a psychiatric ward in a general hospital. This crisis may last for several straight days. Reasons for this "breakdown" in coping commonly include:

- A person is so depressed that she has no energy or motivation to move, even to get out of bed. Suicidal ideas may set in as the depressed individual feels hopeless about getting better.
- The development of acute psychosis may occur. In this case, a person can't distinguish between real and imagined sounds, sights, or smells (**hallucinations**). He has lost his grip on reality and is often convinced of the truth of outrageous ideas (**delusions**). His judgment is severely impaired, and he may become suicidal or homicidal because he hears a voice directing him to do so.
- People with panic disorder sometimes feel they are totally disabled with fear and that they are losing their minds. However distressing, panic attacks are transient events, and are not likely to lead to hospitalization.

The phrase "nerves acting up" is a popular reference to feeling quite anxious, but it does not mean that the nervous system is about to overload or break down. If someone feels overwhelming nervousness and shaking as a result of withdrawal from alcohol or other drugs or medicines, however, she may need to be hospitalized as a medical emergency.

I'm afraid I'm wearing my body out with my panic attacks. Can panic tear up my body?

Obviously, people feel better physically when they are managing their emotional problems well. Whereas prolonged, unmanaged stress is associated with increased health problems, we can't say that panic symptoms "tear up" a person's body. Nerves don't become compromised by frequent panic attacks. Remember, all the symptoms in a panic attack are the result of the fight-or-flight system kicking in through activation of the sympathetic nervous system. The sympathetic nervous system is designed to protect you. Just because this response might be happening more than you want, this doesn't mean that the sympathetic nervous system is going to get worn out, stop working, or hurt other areas of your body. Although unpleasant, frequent panic attacks indicate that your fight-or-flight mechanism is responding to a lot of false alarms—again, a situation that is uncomfortable but still *harmless*.

Also, keep in mind that for every time your sympathetic nervous system gets activated, the parasympathetic nervous system will also kick in. This is the system that opposes, or balances out, the fight-or-flight response, and this mechanism will calm you down. The body is set up so that parasympathetic activity will not let sympathetic activity continue to increase in any kind of unsafe way.

The main message here is that panic is unpleasant enough without your making it worse by assuming that your body is being harmed by it. A thought that can exacerbate your panic symptoms and increase your susceptibility to panic attacks is "Oh my God, I'm ruining my body." This thought is untrue. More helpful self-talk would be "I don't like these symptoms, but I can ride them out and remind myself that they are not harmful to my body."

What is hyperventilation? Can it make me pass out?

Hyperventilation, also known as overbreathing, is breathing at a rate and depth excessive for the current situation. If you were running in a race, an intense breathing pattern would be necessary. If you are sitting at your desk preparing for an important meeting, overbreathing is not necessary. When you hyperventilate, you are breathing too quickly for a few minutes. This results in a change in the balance of oxygen and carbon dioxide in the blood, which can be associated with shortness of breath, numbness, tingling, lightheadedness, dizziness, chest pain, and palpitations. Notably, the main ingredient in hyperventilation is a sudden drop in the carbon dioxide level in the bloodstream, *not* the oxygen level. Keep in mind that hyperventilation may produce some uncomfortable physical symptoms, but it is not dangerous. There is plenty of oxygen in the body, although it is not being used as efficiently—a situation that is *inconvenient but harmless*. Some people notice bodily changes associated with hyperventilation and start to tell themselves, "I can't stand this... I can't breathe." These untrue, catastrophic interpretations increase the emotion of anxiety and worsen physical sensations. A more true statement is that *hyperventilation is unpleasant but not harmful*. In fact, one of the most useful diagnostic and intervention tools in treating panic is called the hyperventilation stress test. Here, in collaboration with a trained therapist, a patient purposefully hyperventilates so:

1. He can see how this breathing pattern produces physical sensations
2. He can learn the sensations aren't dangerous and become less bothered by them
3. He can realize unpleasant symptoms don't mean that his body is out of control.

When a person is hyperventilating, blood pressure and heart rate are elevated. Fainting involves an increase in blood pressure and heart rate followed by an *abrupt decline* in these measures. Although it can feel like you are not getting enough air or that you are going to pass out, it is very unusual for a person to faint because of hyperventilation. In general, people who say they have passed out due to hyperventilation have other tendencies that make them more likely to faint.

I feel like panic has taken over my life. How are other people limited by their panic attacks?

People who struggle with frequent panic attacks are fundamentally afraid of uncomfortable bodily sensations associated with the fight-or-flight reaction. Additionally, they worry that they might humiliate themselves, harm themselves, hurt someone else, vomit in public, lose control of their bladder or bowels, be unable to breathe, go crazy, have a heart attack or stroke, or faint. When a person is terrified of having a panic attack, many places and situations become off-limits in his or her mind. These might include:

Driving	Meetings at work
Riding in a car as a passenger	Elevators/escalators
Grocery stores	Being home alone
Malls	Traveling a long distance from home
Crowds	Unfamiliar places
Movie theaters	Going outside for a walk
Restaurants	Exercise
Buses/subways/planes	Parties
Bridges/tunnels	Drinking caffeine

My friends say they can't tell when I'm having a panic attack, but I know it's got to be so obvious. Can you help me understand this?

When you're having a panic attack, you are intensely focused on the changes that are going on inside your body. Given the uninvited sensations you're experiencing, it's difficult to focus on anything else. Panic symptoms might feel like a tidal wave or a volcano inside of you, so you assume that everyone else must be able to see your intense discomfort. However, this anxiety-increasing assumption is usually untrue. In most cases, we cannot tell when someone is having a panic attack unless they tell us. So, if your friends or family members have indicated that they don't know when you're having a panic attack, it's probably a good idea to believe them. One of the thoughts that can increase people's likelihood of having panic attacks and worsen symptoms during an attack is "It's terrible for other people to see me having a panic attack." Undoubtedly, a belief like this will make you feel more anxious. More helpful, calming self-talk might be, "My friends have said they can't tell when I'm having a panic attack—other people aren't seeing what I'm feeling."

I've heard that you can't have a panic attack if you're relaxed or if you're laughing. Why is that?

Being very relaxed or laughing probably indicates that your mind is not focused on possible threat or danger—and, you're likely to be distracted from your fear of panicking. During a panic attack, your body is centered on and geared up for protecting you from danger (most likely a false alarm). If you're truly relaxed or laughing, however, these states are usually incompatible with the fight-or-flight reaction. Sympathetic nervous system activation (which occurs during a panic attack) involves increased heart rate, increased blood pressure, and increased respiration rate. In contrast, during a genuine state of relaxation (as produced by relaxation induction activities), heart rate, blood pressure, and respiration rate are all decreased.

People often can learn ways of distracting themselves from anticipating and experiencing panic attacks. Doing a relaxation activity or finding an enjoyable activity that promotes laughter might be very helpful. However, it's not a good idea to expect a guarantee or depend on a certain technique to keep from panicking. (How do people cope when one of their "surefire" ways of offsetting panic doesn't work?) Instead, it's more beneficial for individuals to train their minds to believe that panic symptoms aren't dangerous and that it's possible to ride them out. Deliberately bringing on panic symptoms (interoceptive exposure) is one of the best methods for accomplishing this goal.

I've had panic attacks during the day, but recently, I was jolted from sleep and found myself in the middle of a panic attack. Is this normal?

Studies have estimated that anywhere from 45 to 70% of panic disorder sufferers experience nighttime, or *nocturnal*, panic attacks. Nocturnal panic attacks tend to occur a half-hour to three-and-a-half hours after falling asleep, during non-REM (rapid eye movement) sleep. This means that the person is not likely to be dreaming. Nocturnal attacks are distinguished from other nighttime distress, such as waking from a nightmare or a night terror. Although night terrors can share features of nocturnal panic, such as sudden awakening and physical arousal, there are three important differences:

1. People in the midst of a night terror often become verbally and physically active, whereas a panic attack will be unnoticed until the person awakens
2. Night terrors are followed by amnesia, whereas nocturnal panic attacks are vividly remembered
3. Night terror sufferers usually go right back to sleep, whereas the panic sufferer often responds with insomnia

Although nocturnal panic can result in sleep loss and impaired performance the next day, they are no more dangerous than daytime panic attacks.

I try not to go outside too much in the summer because I'm afraid I'll have a panic attack. Can heat make it more likely that I will panic?

People do report more symptoms of panic disorder and agoraphobia during the summer. Being outside in the heat can increase people's heart rate and respiration rate. High temperatures might also produce lightheadedness as well as feelings of dehydration or nausea. Whereas these sensations might be uncomfortable for anyone, they can be especially alarming to someone struggling with panic attacks. Remember, a panic sufferer is already extremely tuned in to noticing any bodily changes and is well-practiced in thinking the worst.

To avoid having a panic attack, individuals might decide to stay inside more during summer, where they feel less vulnerable. The problem with this strategy is that the more the person avoids going outside, the more she builds anticipatory anxiety ("I'll get too hot, I won't be able to breathe, I'll have a panic attack") and increases the chances of having a panic attack when she finally does have to go out into the heat. (We can't very easily avoid ever going outside during the summer months!) Hopefully, you're seeing a theme here by now—with panic (and other anxiety problems), avoidance strategies provide short-term gain but long-term pain! Even if you don't like the bodily changes that go along with being outside in high temperatures, you're better off facing this discomfort and allowing yourself to get used to it than hiding from it. Do you really want to feel trapped in your home until autumn comes?

I've heard that panic attacks can lead to agoraphobia. Why? What is agoraphobia anyway?

Agoraphobia is intense anxiety about being in situations: (a) where you think escape might be very difficult or embarrassing, or (b) where you think you couldn't get help if you needed it. When people are agoraphobic, they tend to avoid places such as grocery stores, the mall, movie theaters, driving in cars, crossing bridges, and going through tunnels. You probably can think of other places that feel scary to you and that you have gotten in the habit of avoiding. Here's how panic attacks can lead to the development of agoraphobia:

1. John goes to the mall and has a panic attack.
2. John then starts thinking, "It's awful to have a panic attack at the mall. How embarrassing! I can't stand those symptoms."
3. Now John associates the mall with panic.
4. Given that John doesn't want to panic again, he decides, "I won't go to the mall anymore."

The problem is this: the more John stays away from the mall, the stronger his fear of the mall becomes. He may also begin to fear other similar places, and to increasingly restrict his life. Meanwhile, he misses the opportunity to see that he can survive panic attacks, even when they do occur in the feared place.

For some people, agoraphobia becomes like a prison. People want to create a safety zone for themselves, so they stay in their home to avoid danger or discomfort. This approach has short-term gain, because people may avoid the unpleasantness of panic outside the home. However, the long-term distress of having life narrowed and restricted is a high price to pay for avoidance of brief discomfort.

Chapter 7

COPING WITH PANIC

- It's hard to think clearly in the midst of a panic attack. What can I do?
- I don't like to talk about my panic attacks because I'm afraid of bringing one on. Is it important that I get treatment for my panic?
- What is the best type of psychotherapy for panic disorder?
- Are there medicines for panic attacks?
- I've heard that it can help to bring on a panic attack. Is this really true?
- Are there specific activities that help people with panic attacks?
- What is diaphragmatic breathing?
- How can I learn to breathe in this slower, deeper manner?
- Relaxation techniques didn't help my panic attacks. Why is that?
- Is there something wrong with having a "safety zone"—a place where I feel comfortable?
- I've heard that my panic attacks aren't dangerous and that it's my thoughts that are keeping me stuck. I don't understand this. I feel like my world is crumbling when I'm having an attack—how am I supposed to think my way out of this?
- I'm afraid to drive because I think my panic symptoms could cause me to lose control of my car and wreck. Is that possible?
- I'd like to exercise but I'm afraid to because I think it will lead to a panic attack. What can I do?
- My daughter has panic attacks and won't drive anywhere on her own. Am I enabling her if I take her to run errands and to her appointments?

It's hard to think clearly in the midst of a panic attack. What can I do?

Understanding what's happening during a panic attack is one of your best tools for getting better. Another huge weapon against panic is allowing yourself to ride out the attack without trying to make it stop. To do this, people benefit from having well-practiced coping statements of which to remind themselves. The following list contains coping thoughts that individuals have found to be helpful during panic attacks. Consider which statements might have the most useful impact on you. It's a good idea to keep this list handy (in your purse, briefcase, or car), or to take a few of the statements and write them down on notecards to keep with you.

- Anxiety is normal.

- It's better to have too much anxiety than not enough.

- Anxiety is designed to protect me, not hurt me.

- These feelings are uncomfortable but not dangerous.

- I've been through countless panic attacks, and they always pass.

- I don't have to make these sensations stop—my body will stop them naturally.

- Anxiety is temporary.

- I'm not having a heart attack or a stroke.

- My heart is designed to beat this fast and faster.

- I'm not going to lose control or go crazy.

- Having unpleasant physical sensations doesn't mean I'm totally out of control.

- I can be anxious and still function.

- Other people can't see what I'm feeling.

- It's not that I don't have enough air—I'm actually overbreathing and there's plenty of air.

I don't like to talk about my panic attacks because I'm afraid of bringing one on. Is it important that I get treatment for my panic?

Panic attacks are associated with many difficulties if left untreated. These difficulties include:

- An increased tendency to use alcohol and other drugs for coping
- More time spent in hospital emergency rooms
- Less time spent on hobbies, sports, and other pleasurable activities
- Increased financial dependence on others
- More emotional and physical difficulties
- An increased fear of driving more than a few miles away from home
- A greater risk of attempting suicide

Obviously panic comes with many costs, so it is a good idea to be willing to discuss your panic disorder with a trained professional and pursue effective treatment. As far as your concern about bringing on a panic attack, let's look at the realities:

1. Fear and avoidance are the best ways to keep the panic in charge. There is much wisdom to the statement, "that which you resist, persists." By entering treatment, you are taking an important step toward reclaiming your life.
2. Disclosing concerns to a professional often brings relief rather than anxiety.
3. Even if the worst-case scenario happened and you had a panic attack, you would be in the best place possible! In fact, you and your therapist would be able to learn more about how your attacks come about and be better equipped to help you.

Even so, you may feel better if you talk to the therapist *before* scheduling your first appointment. Most therapists are willing to talk with you briefly by phone to help you make decisions about your treatment. This is a good way to make sure you are matched with a therapist who has training and experience in treating panic disorder. Further, you may feel more at ease just by knowing that your therapist is aware of your concerns.

What is the best type of psychotherapy for panic disorder?

According to the prevailing research, as well as the recommendations of the National Institute of Mental Health, cognitive-behavioral therapy is the most effective type of therapy for panic disorder. Cognitive-behavioral therapy (CBT) involves: (a) learning to think more realistically, and (b) adjusting your behavior so you can respond more helpfully to your panic symptoms. You can generally expect to be in treatment for about 12 weeks, at one therapy session per week, if you want to improve your panic symptoms. For people who have more severe panic disorder or other co-occurring problems, treatment can take longer. In addition, treatment length—as well as effectiveness—will be impacted by your own motivation and willingness to practice new ways of thinking and behaving. The good news is CBT is very successful for treating panic disorder, with studies demonstrating improvement in 70–90% of patients treated. In addition, treated patients experience few adverse effects and a relatively low relapse rate of panic attacks.

Are there medicines for panic attacks?

In general, two types of medications are used for panic attacks. These include benzodiazepines and antidepressants, both of which have advantages and disadvantages. Benzodiazepines, also known as tranquilizers, can help calm you down so that you feel less keyed up and more relaxed. A benefit of benzodiazepines is that people experience relief relatively quickly. A compelling disadvantage of benzodiazepines, however, is that they can lead to both physical and psychological dependence. This means that people come to rely on medication to decrease their anxiety symptoms instead of learning to deal with anxiety symptoms on their own. Over time, if you become dependent on a medication, you need more and more of it to produce the same beneficial effects. For some people, this can become a huge problem.

Antidepressants, particularly selective serotonin reuptake inhibitors (SSRIs), are also used to treat panic disorder. These medications are taken daily with the idea of helping you decrease your anxiety over time, rather than being taken on an as-needed basis. It is important to be consistent when taking an antidepressant. Advantages of the SSRIs are that they do help with anxiety and people don't usually become psychologically or physically dependent upon them. A problem with SSRIs are that they may produce side effects, which might include headache, nausea, weight gain, or sexual side effects. Another difficulty associated with using SSRIs or other antidepressants for panic disorder is that these medications don't kick in right away. You generally need to allow two to six weeks before the full benefit is experienced. The decision to start medication for panic disorder is an individual one and one you should discuss carefully with your physician or mental health professional. Different people have different preferences. Studies do show, however, that cognitive-behavioral therapy has better long-term results than medication treatment alone.

I've heard that it can help to bring on a panic attack. Is this really true?

This is the idea behind a therapy technique called **interoceptive exposure**. *Interoceptive* means feedback from the body, and *exposure* refers to exposing yourself to this feedback. With this technique, you work on becoming less scared of the symptoms associated with panic by creating the symptoms yourself. One of the hallmarks of panic disorder is anxiety sensitivity—fear of anxiety-related symptoms. In fact, panic is often referred to as "fear of fear" because a person is afraid to experience the sensations produced by the fight-or-flight reaction. However, *this extreme fear of panicking is what allows the disorder to persist*. The more a person tries to avoid the symptoms, the more severe and long-lasting the distress. When people get to the point that they are not terrified of panic attacks and are more willing to have them, then the panic has less power.

With interoceptive exposure, you work with your therapist to bring on the panic symptoms that are disturbing to you. This process is done gradually and collaboratively. It might include:

1. Running up and down stairs to increase your heart rate and produce sweating
2. Quickly breathing through a straw to produce hyperventilation
3. Staring in a mirror to produce a sense of unreality.

Whereas interoceptive exposure might feel uncomfortable at first, it is a great tool for becoming less bothered by your panic symptoms.

To help make this idea clearer, think of unexpectedly seeing a very gory scene from a horror movie when you're walking by the television set. The first time you see the image, you might feel very scared or grossed out (even if you like horror movies). However, if you watched this same scene 100 times, do you think you would be as affected by the image on the 100th viewing? Probably not! This is the idea with interoceptive exposure—you repeatedly expose yourself to initially very unpleasant sensations so that they become less troublesome to you over time. Interoceptive exposure diminishes your anxiety sensitivity, shows you that you do have some control over what happens in your body, and allows you to disprove the horrible things you previously thought about your panic symptoms.

Are there specific activities that help people with panic attacks?

Interoceptive exposure involves facing the panic symptoms you fear and getting used to them without applying calming techniques. By doing so, you learn, "I *can* stand this; it's not going to kill me. I'm not going crazy, I'm not having a heart attack, and I'm not losing control." More than anything, however, you see clearly that bad feelings come and pass. Here are some techniques used in cognitive-behavioral therapy for facing specific panic symptoms (keep in mind that these techniques are done collaboratively and with a clear understanding of the rationale.):

- For the thought "I'm having a heart attack": Use stationary bike, run in place, run up and down stairs, walk outside when it's hot
- For the thought "I can't breathe": Hold breath, breathe through a straw, hyperventilate for at least 60-90 seconds
- For the thought "I'm so dizzy I'm going to faint": Spin in a chair (60 seconds) or shake head from side to side (30 seconds)
- For the thought "It's awful to feel unreal or detached": Hyperventilate, stare at a dot on the wall, or stare at yourself in the mirror for at least 90 seconds
- For the thought "I'm losing control, going crazy": Watch movie clips or read book excerpts that depict scenes of insanity
- For the thought "It would be awful to have a panic attack in public": Pretend to have a panic attack in public, force yourself to run out of a social event

What is diaphragmatic breathing?

Diaphragmatic breathing, also referred to as slow breathing, stomach breathing, or breathing retraining, is a technique used to regulate your breathing habit. Many people who struggle with panic are chronic hyperventilators, meaning they are in the habit of over-breathing. Whereas a normal breathing rate is eight to sixteen breaths per minute, people with panic disorder sometimes breathe up to thirty times per minute. Fast overbreathing makes sense during exercise or sports activities; however, it is not efficient or helpful during normal daily activities like working in an office or going to school. In fact, chronic subtle overbreathing is associated with increased tension in the body as well as other unpleasant physical symptoms. Diaphragmatic breathing is a tool to correct unnecessary overbreathing and promote balance in the oxygen and carbon dioxide levels in your blood.

Diaphragmatic breathing focuses on helping a person learn how to breathe using the diaphragm muscle (large muscle under the lungs) instead of shallow chest muscles. Think about how babies breathe. If you watch a baby sleeping, you will see her stomach going up and down as she inhales and exhales. She is using her diaphragm for breathing, which we were intended to do during normal activities. However, as we grow up, many of us shift to a reliance on our chest muscles for inhaling and exhaling. We do this when we feel tense or stressed. We also become socialized to holding our stomachs in, which promotes less optimal breathing. Over time, shallow chest breathing can become a habit that increases the likelihood of panicking. Diaphragmatic breathing allows for slower, deeper inhalation.

How can I learn to breathe in this slower, deeper manner?

To learn diaphragmatic breathing, keep in mind that this is a skill that requires practice. Meaningful benefits accrue with consistent work on a regular basis. Remember, diaphragmatic breathing is intended to help you change your habitual breathing pattern. Although slow breathing can help you feel better if you are having a panic attack, you don't want to rely on using diaphragmatic breathing to control panic on an acute basis. Any focus on stopping, avoiding, or resisting panic symptoms is likely to strengthen them over time. Diaphragmatic breathing is not a quick fix, but rather a lifestyle change.

Use this practice routine to learn diaphragmatic breathing:

1. Find a quiet, comfortable environment where you won't be interrupted.
2. Decide whether you would prefer to sit in a chair or lie on a bed. Some people prefer to close their eyes.
3. Make sure you are wearing comfortable, loose-fitting clothing.
4. Place your right hand on the center of your stomach.
5. Place your left hand on your upper chest (over your sternum).
6. Inhale through your nose on the count of four.
7. While inhaling, push your stomach out so that you feel your right hand moving up. Pretend you are blowing up a balloon in your stomach and that the air is coming in through your nose down an imaginary path to your stomach.
8. Exhale on the count of four by letting air out through pursed lips. Imagine gently letting air out of the pretend balloon in your stomach, not forcing it. You should feel your right hand going down as your stomach contracts.
9. Be mindful that the left hand over the chest should move less than the right hand over the stomach.

10. Repeat this process for 10 minutes. If it feels awkward, remind yourself that any new skill requires practice and that this technique will help you to manage your anxiety better over time.
11. Schedule times to practice this technique at least once, but preferably twice, per day.

Relaxation techniques didn't help my panic attacks. Why is that?

Different people respond differently to doing relaxation induction activities. For some individuals, calming their body through progressive muscle relaxation, imagery, or visualization is a great way to reduce tension and improve responses to stress. For other people, however, structured relaxation induction or deliberate "quiet-time" activities can actually promote more of a focus on bodily changes, which might increase the likelihood of having a panic attack. Here's an example: A man who suffers from panic attacks goes to work, performs at his stressful bank job for ten hours, endures the one-hour commute home, eats dinner with his family, and mows the lawn—all without panicking. After this long, demanding day, he decides to "chill out" by reading a book while sitting in his recliner in the quiet setting of his home den—interestingly, this is the time he experiences a panic attack! Why? Because all throughout the day, this individual was focused on tasks he needed to complete and not so focused on bodily fluctuations. It was only when he sat down in his recliner that he started to notice that his heart seemed to be beating faster than he considered normal. Once he made this quick observation about his heart rate, he automatically thought, "Oh no—something's wrong!" which caused his heart to beat faster and brought about shortness of breath, leading to more negative explanations for these symptoms, and so on.

Is there something wrong with having a "safety zone"—a place where I feel comfortable?

A safety zone or behavior is anything that a person uses to say, "I'll be okay as long as I _____" (stay in a certain area, go with a certain person, have a certain object, do a certain behavior, etc.). Safety zones and safety behaviors provide relief and reassurance for a panic sufferer in the moment—however, they are not good long-term strategies. Inevitably, safety behaviors lose their effectiveness, and they generally make your life more restricted. Here are some examples of safety behaviors:

- Staying in a safe zone (usually one's home)
- Making sure you're with a safe person (mother, husband, etc.)
- Keeping a pill bottle with you
- Carrying a cell phone wherever you go
- Having your husband drive behind you when you go to work
- Making sure you always have a beverage with you
- Always driving on the slower roads vs. the interstate
- Using distractions (e.g., turning the volume of the radio up, singing, etc.)
- Reassurance-seeking

To really beat your panic symptoms, you need to show yourself that the sensations are temporary and harmless, and that you can stand them. The more you avoid facing panic feelings through the use of safety behaviors, the less you get to observe the panic symptoms with a more realistic perspective. Safety behaviors allow you to hold onto your catastrophic predictions about harmless physical fluctuations. Keep in mind that avoidance is anxiety's best friend, and safety behaviors are an excellent form of avoidance. Safety behaviors keep you from giving yourself the credit for managing your anxiety—instead, you give your credit to being at home, having your cell phone with you, carrying your pill bottle, or other safety behavior. Note that we are not saying it's always bad to have help—you just want to make sure you gradually phase out these safety cues so that you can feel better about your ability to deal with your panic symptoms on your own. You can work toward carrying a sense of safety within you, through reassuring self-talk and your own feelings of strength, rather than relying on restrictive safety behaviors.

I've heard that my panic attacks aren't dangerous and that it's my thoughts that are keeping me stuck. I don't understand this. I feel like my world is crumbling when I'm having an attack—how am I supposed to think my way out of this?

Having panic attacks can feel terrifying—nobody would expect you to "just think" your way out of them. However, understanding what comprises panic attacks and practicing more helpful responses to them are likely to help you. Panic has been described as "fear of fear"—basically, people become quite frightened of the symptoms associated with their body's fear or emergency reaction. This can happen very automatically. From the time of your first panic attack, when you probably had absolutely no idea what was happening to you, it is likely you began telling yourself some very upsetting things about the symptoms—"I can't stand this; This is awful; I can't go through that again; Please God, don't let me panic; I'm going crazy, I can't function this way." Perhaps with each subsequent attack, you have also had this same kind of automatic internal dialogue. It is these thoughts *plus* the symptoms, not just the symptoms themselves, that maintain panic disorder.

Paradoxically, the more you resist panic attacks, the more you are likely to have them. Dreading panic attacks (which comes from what you tell yourself) actually gives the attacks more power over you; in contrast, when you are willing to have panic attacks, you get more power over them. Therefore, developing more realistic, balanced coping self-talk is beneficial (e.g., "I don't like this, but I can stand it; This is very uncomfortable but not awful; I don't want to panic again, but if I do, I can handle it; Having panic attacks does not mean I'm going crazy; Even when I'm panicking, I can still function"). Thoughts don't change easily, but practicing saying accurate, helpful statements to yourself does help you manage problems better.

We've talked a lot about thoughts related to panic symptoms—understanding this link is crucial. However, keep in mind that a "conditioned association effect" also occurs with panic symptoms and scared feelings. Through repeated panic attacks, you may have learned to associate a feeling of terror with your heart racing and shortness of breath. Now, any time your heart races or you feel short of breath, a feeling of terror arises. This connection might feel ingrained and inevitable to you at this point. However, an important part of getting better from panic is breaking the link between the feelings of terror and the bodily symptoms. You can do this in therapy by deliberately producing the symptoms and letting your feeling of terror come and pass—the panic symptoms will eventually subside, and the scary emotion will pass! The more you actively produce the symptoms and allow your body to become desensitized to them, the less terror you will feel. You can still feel annoyed and uncomfortable about the bodily fluctuations associated with a panic attack, but working hard to get rid of the terror and dread will provide great benefits to you in the long-run. Ultimately, genuine relief from panic comes from eliminating the fear of panic attacks through more accurate self-talk and exposure to the panic symptoms.

I'm afraid to drive because I think my panic symptoms could cause me to lose control of my car and wreck. Is that possible?

Many people are afraid to drive because they believe that panic symptoms will undermine their ability to operate their car. Here is another case where *feelings aren't facts*. Even though panic sensations might lead you to feel out of control or that you can't concentrate, you are still very much in control and you can still concentrate. Remember, panic comes from our body's protection system reacting to false danger alarms. When mechanisms that were designed to protect us arise unexpectedly and unnecessarily, this can be distracting and unpleasant; however, these symptoms are not dangerous. Sympathetic nervous system activation means the body is mobilized for action. While the panic-affected body might prefer that this action be escaping or avoiding the current situation, a person is still able to drive a car in the midst of a panic attack. The bottom line here is that a panic attack in the car can be very scary and distracting, but you can still operate your vehicle without increased risk of hurting yourself or others. The best way to know this is to make yourself practice driving.

The more a person avoids driving, the more the catastrophic interpretations become embedded, which can worsen panic symptoms.

I'd like to exercise but I'm afraid to because I think it will lead to a panic attack. What can I do?

As long as your physician approves, the best thing would be to begin exercising gradually. The longer you avoid exercising, the longer you will stay afraid. Remember that *avoidance is anxiety's best friend*. The most effective way to become less fearful of exercise (or anything, for that matter) is to face the fear. Also, keep in mind that you're probably not anxious about exercising in and of itself; rather, you're anxious about having a panic attack during exercise. But, the more you try to insist that you don't panic in any of your daily activities, the greater the chances of panicking. People who struggle with panic tend to be more sensitive to and focused on any changes in bodily sensations. Further, when they notice a fluctuation (e.g., faster heart rate, sweating, shakiness), they make a very negative interpretation of it (e.g., "I'm going to have a heart attack; I can't stand this; I'm going to die; I'm going to lose control; My body can't handle this"). It is the combination of harmless physical sensations and catastrophic self-talk about the physical sensations that produces and maintains panic attacks.

By beginning to exercise gradually, you would be doing yourself a favor on several levels. First, you would get to see that your catastrophic beliefs about physical fluctuations are untrue. Even if your heart was racing and you were sweating profusely, you would not die, lose control, or go crazy. You would find that even if you had a panic attack, you could still function during the exercise and ride out the panic attack. Second, you would be exposing yourself to the very symptoms that you fear—an excellent step. The more you experienced your heart racing, sweatiness, shakiness, etc., the more you would become desensitized to these sensations. Over time, they would bother you less. A recent study showed that low-intensity walking reduced anxiety sensitivity, but high-intensity exercise produced even better results. Third, countless studies have shown that exercise is beneficial for reducing stress and depression.

When beginning an exercise program, it's a good idea to keep track of your progress with your fitness as well as with your mood. Written data that show the exercises are getting easier and that your symptom discomfort is improving can be a great motivator for continued exercise.

My daughter has panic attacks and won't drive anywhere on her own. Am I enabling her if I take her to run errands and to her appointments?

It probably isn't helpful to call yourself an enabler. Presumably, you are helping your daughter because you love her and she is asking for assistance with transportation. Undoubtedly, you don't want to see her suffer further by your refusing to take her where she needs to go. However, family members do better when they can find a balance between helping a loved one and not accommodating or promoting her anxiety symptoms. Be careful not to strengthen your daughter's anticipatory anxiety by indefinitely allowing her to avoid the symptoms and situations she fears. Asking yourself the following questions may help you sort out how to respond to your daughter's requests:

- How distressing is it to you to take your daughter to these places?
- Are you willing to arrange workable compromises with her so that you can feel better about your driving role and she can begin taking more responsibility for herself?
- If you don't want to transport her, what are you telling yourself that gets you to go ahead and take her? Perhaps you're thinking that she can't handle your not giving her a ride or that it would be awful if she didn't get where she needed to be. In contrast, your not driving her to all her desired destinations might be inconvenient instead of awful. Further, it may provide some motivation for her to seek treatment.

Chapter 8

UNDERSTANDING PHOBIAS

- What is the difference between a fear and a phobia?
- How do phobias develop?
- What are the most common types of phobias?
- How many different kinds of phobias exist? What are some of the more unusual ones?
- Are all phobias treated in the same way? If so, what is the standard treatment?
- What is an exposure hierarchy?
- What is an example of an exposure hierarchy?
- Can I be hypnotized to get rid of my phobia?
- I'm afraid of certain animals and situations. How do I know if I have a phobia?
- What is the difference between a superstition and a phobia?
- I heard that you can use virtual reality for treating phobias! How does that work?

What is the difference between a fear and a phobia?

We feel fear when we are concerned about being harmed. Fear motivates us to avoid what we're scared of. A fear can be reasonable, meaning there actually is a risk of harm, or unreasonable, meaning most people wouldn't be concerned if they were in that situation. If you step out on your porch and see a poisonous snake coming toward you, yelling and running back in the house would be understandable, even smart. On the other hand, if someone shows you a photo of a poisonous snake, your reaction of screaming and running away may be harder to understand. The latter reaction is evidence of a snake phobia. In both cases, you have an immediate reaction to a specific stimulus or situation, which serves to get you away from the source of "harm." Here's what makes a fear a phobia:

1. It's unreasonable (e.g., reaction to photo of snake) or excessive (e.g., worrying about encountering a snake).

AND

2. You know your fear is unreasonable or excessive, but this knowledge doesn't relieve the fear.

AND

3. Your life is disrupted by the need to avoid the feared object or situation (e.g., you are unable to go to the playground with your children for fear of encountering a snake).

How do phobias develop?

A phobia can develop in response to one or more of the following circumstances:

1. Experiencing a traumatic event. For example, you may fear flying after a very rough, bumpy flight or fear driving after being in a car accident.
2. Witnessing a traumatic event. In this scenario, a person watching the aftermath of a plane crash on television may then become afraid to fly. A child growing up with a mom who is terrified of mice may develop a fear of mice as well. This is also known as **observational learning** or **modeling**.
3. Phobias can also develop as a result of the brain pairing certain stimuli with scared feelings, which is called **classical conditioning**. For example, a person can mentally pair frightened feelings with dogs, snakes, bees, spiders, storms, elevators, or tunnels.

In general, three themes underlie most specific phobias. These include the fear of injury, harm, or death; the fear of being trapped or losing control because you are trapped; and fears of something strange, unusual, or unexpected.

What are the most common types of phobias?

Because phobias are diagnosed by category rather than specific names, we do not have a long, organized list of phobias from the most to least common. Social phobia, estimated to affect between 3 and 13% of the population, would probably be more common than any of the individual specific phobias (e.g., claustrophobia, arachnophobia). As a category, specific phobia has been estimated to affect between 7.2 and 11.3% of the population. Of the specific phobias, the fear of dogs, or cynophobia, seems to be the most frequent. Agoraphobia is almost always diagnosed with panic disorder, and panic disorder has been estimated to affect between 1 and 3.5% of the population.

As far as fears are concerned, surveys have found public speaking to be the most common. While public speaking fear can constitute a social phobia, this is only the case when the fear disrupts the person's functioning or causes marked distress. Most people who fear public speaking just don't do it.

How many different kinds of phobias exist? What are some of the more unusual ones?

A man who is very interested in this question—Fredd Culbertson—has made a hobby of gathering and listing phobia names. As of this writing, Culbertson has identified about 530 phobias, all of which are listed on phobialist.com. His collection, which has been gathered from reference books and medical papers, is a popular resource. The phobias are listed alphabetically, from *ablutophobia*, the fear of washing and bathing, to *zoophobia*, the fear of animals. Here are some of the more unusual ones:

- Arachibutyrophobia, the fear of peanut butter sticking to the roof of the mouth

- Bogyphobia, the fear of the bogeyman
- Cenophobia or Centophobia, the fear of new things or ideas
- Philimaphobia, the fear of kissing
- Soceraphobia, the fear of parents-in-law
- Xanthophobia, the fear of the color or word "yellow"

Keep in mind that just about anything can constitute a phobia if it is the focus of (a) excessive or unreasonable fear that (b) results in avoidance as well as (c) lowered functioning or severe distress. A phobia may seem unusual until you understand a person's history and how the object or situation became associated with danger.

Are all phobias treated in the same way? If so, what is the standard treatment?

The most widely accepted treatment for phobias is exposure therapy. Exposure therapy can occur imaginally (through imagining what you fear) or in vivo (through directly facing the actual stimulus or situation). The benefits of repeated exposure to a feared stimulus to produce habituation have been described earlier. Again, exposure helps people to be less bothered by things that originally frightened them. In facing the dreaded object or situation, it is important to use gradual steps that promote the development of a sense of mastery over fears. Research has shown that desensitization to fear is more profound if the person allows herself to feel anxiety at each step in the exposure process and to let it diminish naturally rather than trying to distract from or resist it.

The following is an example of how exposure therapy might occur. If you have a fear of bridges, your treatment might begin with reading about bridges or watching movie clips containing bridges. At first, you would likely feel some anxiety in doing this. However, as long as you forced yourself to keep looking at the bridge images, your anxiety would subside over time. Once you're comfortable doing these activities, you would proceed to more difficult tasks such as imagining yourself driving over a bridge or walking on one. Again, immersing yourself in these imagined scenarios would produce anxiety that would decline as long as you continued imagining the scenes. When this imaginal work no longer produces distress, it might be time to face real-life bridges. Your assignments might include going to look at a bridge, then riding with your husband across a small bridge, then you driving across a small bridge, and gradually working up to more challenging bridge experiences.

The key here is facing your fears! Exposure therapy has become standard for the treatment of phobias due to the excellent research base to support it.

What is an exposure hierarchy?

The key to conquering any phobia is gradually exposing yourself to what you fear. Regardless of why the phobia developed (and there were probably several contributors involved), a phobic reaction was learned, and therefore can be unlearned. Research suggests that people do better when they face their fear in steps (think of a ladder) and continuously see that they have mastered an aspect of their fear. When participating in cognitive-behavioral therapy, you and your therapist work together to design the steps that you will take in facing your fear. With graded exposure therapy, the idea is to start with more manageable aspects of your feared stimulus and work up to more challenging tasks. It's often helpful to write the needed steps on note cards, and then work with your therapist to order the items from least difficult to most difficult.

When using exposure hierarchies, therapists have people keep track of their **Subjective Units of Distress (SUDs level)**. This self-reported number ranges from 0 (no distress/tension/fear at all) to

100 (most distress/tension/fear ever). During exposure, a client's SUDs levels are assessed as she faces each hierarchy item. To achieve habituation, or desensitization, to each feared item, it is necessary for the client to stay in that particular situation until the SUDs level has gone down by at least half.

What is an example of an exposure hierarchy?

Here is an example of a hierarchy that might be developed for an elevator phobia, with step one representing the least anxiety-provoking step, and step eleven representing the most-feared experience:

1. Read about elevators and look at pictures of them.
2. Watch television/movie clips of people riding in elevators.
3. Observe real people riding up and down in elevators.
4. With a family member, get on and off elevator leaving door open.
5. With a family member, stand in closed elevator.
6. With a family member, ride up one floor and down one floor.
7. With family member, gradually increase number of floors traveled.
8. Stand in elevator alone with door closed.
9. Ride up and down one floor in elevator alone.
10. Continue riding in elevator alone, increasing the floors traveled each time.
11. Practice at least one elevator ride alone per day for several weeks.

Can I be hypnotized to get rid of my phobia?

While hypnosis may be used to treat a phobia, the process does not magically "get rid of" phobias. People vary in their ability to be hypnotized. There is evidence that people who are more suscepti-ble to developing phobias are also susceptible to hypnosis and therefore make good candidates for the treatment. Hypnotherapy addresses phobias by replacing the association between the stimu-lus (e.g., heights, bridges, flying, getting shots) and anxiety with feelings of security, courage and confidence. The concept of expo-sure therapy is included in hypnosis by having the client imagine the steps in the exposure hierarchy rather than physically going through each step. Hypnosis and self-hypnosis are also used to pro-mote relaxation in the face of phobic stimuli. There are many sim-ilarities between relaxation and hypnosis—in fact, the hypnotic state is said to be a state of deep relaxation. Research comparing self-hypnosis with relaxation found that subjects using self-hypnosis felt more satisfied and confident with the technique as a way of managing their anxiety than those using relaxation, though both approaches were effective.

Keep in mind that the idea that hypnosis puts you "out" while somebody else fixes you is a myth. The hypnotherapy client remains conscious, and the therapy is considered a collaborative effort rather than a performance by a magician.

I'm afraid of certain animals and situations. How do I know if I have a phobia?

If you and most of the people in your life would agree that your fear is excessive or unreasonable, you may have a phobia. If you are terrified of being in the company of wild bears even though sometimes people can be in their company without harm, your fear is still considered more than reasonable. On the other hand, if you are terrified of all dogs, where the odds of being attacked are relatively small and the rewards of spending time with them are high, this may be an irrational fear. Adults with phobias are aware of the irrational nature of their fears, yet this awareness does not help diminish the fear.

People with phobias experience distress and sometimes panic when they *face* the feared stimulus. They also become agitated and anxious when they expect the *possibility* of encountering what they fear. We call this **anticipatory anxiety**. Finally, phobias are generally characterized by avoidance of the feared object or situation. For example, if you have a dog phobia, you may refuse to visit friends with pet dogs and only frequent places that restrict dogs.

What is the difference between a superstition and a phobia?

A phobia is an intense and irrational fear of an object or situation. An example is the fear of bridges. Falling off a bridge can be lethal, but the chances of doing so are slim. *The phobic knows his fear is irrational.* He just can't control his fearful reaction. If the stimulus or situation that is feared is a common element in the phobic's life, his life may become dysfunctional, and his distress level will be high.

A superstition is a common but false belief or practice that may involve fear or hope. It is usually based on ignorance, magic or belief in the supernatural. Examples of superstitions include the belief that bad luck comes to the person whose path is crossed by a black cat or to someone who breaks a mirror. Although the belief is irrational and not based on evidence, it is believed by the person holding the superstition. The superstitious individual may go out of his way to avoid the events he fears or to bring about the events he wants. If the superstition is unique to the individual and not shared by others, it may be called a delusion—a false belief that does not stand up to logic or evidence *and* is not commonly shared.

I heard that you can use virtual reality for treating phobias! How does that work?

Given that exposure therapy has been repeatedly demonstrated as effective in the treatment of phobias, it has been a natural step to use advances in technology to increase the sophistication of the exposure. For some phobias, you can gradually face the fear in a pretty straightforward way. For example, if you have a dog phobia, you can look at pictures of dogs, watch movie clips of dogs, watch others pet dogs, look at a dog while standing at the edge of the park, slowly move closer to the dog, try petting the dog, etc. For other fears, it is significantly more difficult and/or costly to face the fear. One instance includes flying. It is logistically complicated and expensive to take multiple flights to desensitize yourself to the fear of flying. What about a storm phobia? We can't make Mother Nature deliver a thunderstorm on demand. Sometimes, it can also be difficult to gather a group of people together to facilitate exposure for public speaking anxiety.

Traditionally, these constraints have primarily been worked around through the use of imaginal exposure. In imaginal exposure, you imagine the feared object, situation, or memories as vividly as possible to evoke the fear cues and promote habituation. Whereas imaginal exposure is still very useful and effective, with certain fears, virtual reality technology may be particularly helpful. Here, a client wears a visor that contains the visual images and sounds of the feared situation. With flying, for example, simulations occur for sitting on the runway, taxiing, taking off, flying in good weather, flying in bad weather, and landing. Virtual reality simulations also exist for thunderstorm, public speaking, and height phobias. As long as you allow yourself to become immersed in the virtual reality scenario, activation of the fear memory and physiological arousal are likely to occur. Habituation, or desensitization, results when you allow yourself to stay with the scenario until your arousal level decreases by at least 50%. Over repeated exposures, anxious symptoms decline and you learn corrective information about your previously embedded irrational fear. So far, several studies suggest that virtual reality therapy is extremely effective.

Chapter 9

MORE ON SPECIFIC PHOBIAS

■ What are some examples of specific phobias?

■ Can medication help with specific phobias?

■ What is claustrophobia, and how is it treated?

■ I have a hard time understanding my sister's fear of flying. She has a successful career that requires long-distance travel, and her husband loves to travel. Can phobias really lead reasonable people to ruin their lives?

■ How can I get past my fear of flying?

■ I haven't been to the dentist in four years because I'm so terrified of being back in that chair and feeling trapped. What can I do about this?

■ What can I tell myself to have the courage to go to the dentist?

■ I have heard that approaching a phobia gradually can help. How might I approach my driving phobia?

■ What is school phobia?

■ I have power struggles with my son every morning because he doesn't want to go to school. He seems really afraid. What should I do?

■ I get a little freaked out when Friday the 13th is coming up. Is Friday the 13th unlucky?

What are some examples of specific phobias?

According to DSM-IV, the diagnostic manual used by mental health professionals, specific phobias are classified into the following five types:

1. **Animal type** includes fears of animals such as snakes, mice, insects, and spiders. These phobias generally begin in childhood, and often disappear as the child matures.
2. **Natural environment type** includes fears of heights, storms, fire, water or natural events such as thunderstorms, hurricanes, tornados, or earthquakes.
3. **Blood/injection/injury type** includes fear of the sight of blood or seeing someone injured. People who have blood/injection/injury phobia are afraid of getting a shot or other invasive medical procedures. Unlike other phobias and most other anxiety disorders, blood/injection/injury phobia does carry with it the possibility of fainting. Fainting occurs because of a sudden increase in blood pressure and heart rate, followed by a sudden decrease in blood pressure and heart rate. In most other problems with anxiety, blood pressure and heart rate are elevated and are not followed by an abrupt decline in these measures.
4. **Situational type** includes an assortment of situations such as flying, elevators, driving, riding on a bus, going through a tunnel or over a bridge, or being in certain areas like shopping malls or restaurants.
5. **Other** is a category for specific phobias that don't fall into the previous four categories. Included here is the fear of open spaces, fear of developing an illness, or fear of certain foods.

The most common types of phobias among adults are situational and natural environment type; for children, natural environment and animal phobias are common.

The prevalence of specific phobias in the general population is about 9%. Over one's lifetime, the expectancy of having a phobia is about 10–11%.

Can medication help with specific phobias?

Medications are not generally recommended for specific phobias. Antidepressants may be useful with the treatment of panic disorder, agoraphobia, social phobia, obsessive-compulsive disorder, and post-traumatic stress disorder, but they do not seem to be that helpful with a specific phobia. Instead, the recommended treatment is cognitive-behavioral therapy (CBT). With CBT, you learn to face your fears so that you are not as terrified of the stimulus. Exposure therapy—or gradually exposing yourself to the feared object—is considered the key to managing a phobia. Regarding medication, it is important to mention that medication can be helpful when a patient initially feels too anxious to do the exposure work without it. However, medication is not a substitute for learning anxiety man-agement skills or for going through the process of desensitization to the feared stimulus. When you think about it, if you rely on a med-ication to get through flying or a public speech, then what you've learned is that you are fine as long as you have the medication. What happens when you don't have it? People develop greater confidence in their ability to manage a phobia when they don't use medication.

What is claustrophobia, and how is it treated?

Approximately 2 out of 100 adults are claustrophobic. Here, a person dreads feeling trapped or closed in and worries about the lack of an easy escape route. When dealing with claustrophobia, you notice the air around you feeling hot and stale; you begin to feel like you can't take satisfying breaths, you start to think, "the walls are closing in on me." People with claustrophobia dread warm, smothering feelings and go out of their way to avoid places where these might occur—elevators, crowded movie theaters, small busy stores, medical testing situations, parties, and full cars or buses. When severe claustrophobia is untreated, the person might become more and more withdrawn from others. However, given that claustrophobia is a learned response (even if other biological or psychological factors contribute), then this uncomfortable, debilitating response can be unlearned.

Similar to the treatment of other phobias, exposure to the fear is the hallmark of effective intervention. Developing more realistic self-talk and learning anxiety management techniques (relaxation procedures, breathing retraining) are also beneficial.

Anxious self-talk for claustrophobia:

I'm trapped—I've got to get out of here!

I can't breathe!

I can't stand this!

I can't have a panic attack in front of all these people!

Coping self-talk for claustrophobia:

I'm not trapped—I'm choosing to face this fear.

There is plenty of air.

I am standing this—it will get easier the more I let myself see that I can do it.

I don't want to panic, but so what if I do? Most likely, nobody would know!

I have a hard time understanding my sister's fear of flying. She has a successful career that requires long-distance travel, and her husband loves to travel. Can phobias really lead reasonable people to ruin their lives?

True phobias do not merely generate uneasiness or apprehension—they generate absolute terror and panic. The sufferer is perfectly aware of the irrational nature of the fear, yet unable to modify it. To understand her distress, imagine being told that your work required you to put your hand over a lit candle for several minutes, and that everyone else was doing it. After a few painful brushes over the flame, you become panicked about the idea of going to work. You start avoiding that painful fate. The phobic reacts as if she were in dire peril much as if she were burning herself. She may also feel foolish for having this intense fear. Phobias can lead to a great deal of impairment in life and can be chronic if not treated. The best way to help your sister is to accept that her distress is real, while letting her know that effective treatment is available.

How can I get past my fear of flying?

If your worries keep you from flying, you are probably suffering from **aviophobia**—the phobia of flying. In deciding what to do, it is a good idea to assess your motivation for flying. You can do this through a cost/benefit analysis in which you list on paper the advantages and disadvantages of the two options, which are flying or not flying. Developing a clear sense of the pros and cons of each of your choices can help you decide whether or not you want to pursue the necessary steps to get more comfortable with flying.

If your fear is that the plane is going to crash and you know that flying is the safest form of transportation, it may be that you aren't really choosing to trust the facts. Here, a choice is very necessary because you will have to decide to believe what the evidence about flying says.

Knowing some data may help you (Source: anxieties.com):

- Your chances of dying in a plane crash are about 1 in 7,000,000.
- When the training hours are summed, pilots have as much education and practice as medical doctors.
- For every hour in the air, a plane receives an average of 12 hours of maintenance.
- Planes are built to withstand for more extreme turbulence than Mother Nature could ever deliver.

The facts support that you are much safer in an airplane than you are in a car. This may be hard to believe because of the media attention that plane crashes generate. Car accidents happen throughout this country every day. They often don't make the papers, but anytime a plane crash occurs, it's in the newspapers, it's on television—it's everywhere. This media attention can lead you to believe that planes are more likely to crash than they actually are. You can't have a guarantee that any form of transportation will be 100% safe, but planes have about the best safety ratings you can get when compared with alternative transportation. You have to decide whether to go with the facts or your emotional reasoning that the plane will crash.

If you want to fly, you'll do best by gradually exposing yourself to stimuli associated with flying, and eventually getting on a plane and flying. You may benefit from one of the many programs that help you gradually approach your fear of flying in a class setting and eventually take a supervised flight with your treatment class. Another good option is virtual reality exposure therapy for flight phobia.

I haven't been to the dentist in four years because I'm so terrified of being back in that chair and feeling trapped. What can I do about this?

First, decide if want to face your dental phobia—if you think it's in your best interest to do so. You may list the advantages and disadvantages of going to the dentist and not going to the dentist. You will probably see the advantages of not going are very short-term in that you delay some possible temporary discomfort. However, the disadvantages of not going are probably far more long-term. Ask yourself, "How important is it to make sure my teeth are healthy?" Are you willing to withstand some temporary discomfort to keep your teeth in good shape? If you answer "yes" to this question, here are some tips to help you get into that chair:

1. Figure out what you are telling yourself about going to the dentist. Are you saying "I'll be trapped" or "I can't stand the pain"? Question these thoughts. Is it really true that you'd be trapped? No! If you told the dentist you wanted to get up out of your chair, he'd let you up. Is it true you can't stand the pain? First, you don't know that there will be pain, and second, if you couldn't stand something, you would die, which is not the case when people go to the dentist.
2. Develop some coping statements for attending your appointment, such as reminding yourself of the benefits of dental care.
3. As with most fears, however, ultimately this fear is decreased by actually going to the dentist. If you want to expose yourself to this situation, you can do this gradually by letting your dentist know that you have a problem with this issue. Many dentists will let people come to the office, sit in the chair, and view the instruments—in other words, practice in preparation for future real visits. By exposing yourself to increasingly challenging tasks,

you will allow habituation to occur, which will help you feel less anxious about the entire experience.

4. Once you are at the dentist's office, keep in mind that distracting yourself is a viable option. Some dentists' offices are equipped with distraction aids such as earphones for listening to music. People can also practice relaxation, visualization, or meditation techniques that they can use when they are actually in the chair having dental procedures done.

What can I tell myself to have the courage to go to the dentist?

Here are some coping statements you may find useful:

- No one particularly wants to go to the dentist, but it is generally better to go ahead and get it over with than to not do it at all.
- Today's dentists are more skilled in dealing with dental procedures, and field advances have made the procedures less painful.
- The Novocain shot only hurts a little bit, and then the pain goes away.
- The dentist will take care of my teeth so that I will have them for years to come.
- Seeing the dentist now will prevent potential pain later.
- I will feel better when I finish my dental appointment, and less worried about the condition of my teeth.

Using more realistic self-statements is an important factor in feeling better about a visit to the dentist. To custom-design self-statements, start with your specific fear, then write a more realistic statement or counter-argument. For example, if you fear being trapped in the chair, tell yourself: "I will not be trapped. The dentist will stop and let me get up at any time."

I have heard that approaching a phobia gradually can help. How might I approach my driving phobia?

1. Sit in car for five minutes alone with ignition turned off.
2. Sit in car for five minutes alone with ignition turned on.
3. Ride in car as a passenger on a drive through the neighborhood.
4. Ride in car as a passenger through downtown area.
5. Ride in car as a passenger on interstate.
6. Drive in neighborhood with family member/friend in car.
7. Drive one block alone.
8. Drive several blocks in neighborhood alone, making right and left turns.
9. Drive downtown with family member in car as passenger.
10. Drive downtown to specified location alone.
11. Drive on interstate with family member in car as passenger.
12. Drive alone on interstate in the right lane, get off on first ramp.
13. Drive alone on the interstate and change lanes; get off at the third ramp.
14. And so on.

As the previous task becomes manageable and 50% less anxiety-provoking, keep working up the hierarchy. You want to feel little distress with an item before moving on to the next more challenging step.

What is school phobia?

A great many children prefer to skip school rather than attend, at least occasionally. However, school phobia, now more commonly referred to as school refusal behavior, can become a debilitating pattern for some children. According to the Anxiety Disorders Association of America, this problem affects 2–5% of school-aged children. Peak difficult times occur between the ages of 5–6 and 10–11. School refusal behavior may also be more apparent after school vacations or summer break.

School refusal behavior is a serious problem, but it can be treated! Facilitating a child's avoidance of school is one of the most unhelpful things parents can do, however. The more a child avoids school, the more his negative beliefs become entrenched. By getting out of school, a child builds up more anticipatory anxiety. Further, he doesn't get to test out his negative predictions to see that things aren't as bad as he thinks..

I have power struggles with my son every morning because he doesn't want to go to school. He seems really afraid. What should I do?

Few things seem more troubling in the midst of a hectic morning than your child refusing to go to school. Our natural tendency is to get upset and yell at our children to make them behave. However, getting into heated battles with your child about school attendance issues (especially during busy mornings) is probably not the best approach to getting your child in school. It is better shift your focus to investigating what is driving your child's school refusal behavior, and then to use problem-solving skills to help your child face his fear.

First, figure out what your child is afraid of. Talk about it when you're both relaxed, perhaps while sharing a pleasurable activity. Keep in mind that the focus of the fear is not the same for all children. Some kids are afraid of their teacher yelling at them, some are afraid of making a bad grade on a test, some are afraid of getting bullied, and some are afraid that they won't see their mother later if they leave her for the whole day. If you have an idea of what your child is telling himself to feel anxious, you're more able to help. Also watch for physical symptoms of anxiety—insomnia, headaches, stomachaches, nausea, and diarrhea.

Make it easy for school personnel—the child's teacher, counselor, and principal—to help your child by providing information about your child's difficulties with anxiety. Let them know how much you value their assistance in improving the school refusal behavior and your child's well-being. Work together! Here are some approaches that can help get your child back in school:

1. Try a gradual approach—perhaps having the child go for part of the day and moderately increasing the time spent at school each week.
2. Some children do very well when they ease into the school day—perhaps spending a few minutes in the gym or in the counselor's office before going into the classroom.
3. Provide your child with encouraging notes or family photos that let him know you're thinking of him and will see him later that afternoon.
4. Teach the child anxiety management skills, such as relaxation or deep breathing.
5. To increase your child's motivation, develop a reward menu and follow through on it predictably and consistently.

I get a little freaked out when Friday the 13th is coming up. Is Friday the 13th unlucky?

Expert Donald Dossey estimates that 17 to 21 million people in the U.S. suffer from **paraskevidekatriaphobia**—or the fear of Friday the 13th (the fear of the number 13 is **triskaidekaphobia**). Yet, many of us are unaware of how Friday the 13th came to be seen as unlucky:

- According to a Norse myth, 12 gods were having a dinner party when the uninvited 13th guest, Loki, arrived. Loki arranged the murder of Balder the Beautiful, the god of joy and gladness. When Balder died, the Earth became dark and mourned.
- The word Friday is named after the Norse goddess, Frigg, the goddess of love and fertility, and grieving mother of Balder. Frigg was banished to the mountains, where she joined 12 witches, transforming them into a coven.
- Judas Iscariot, the betrayer, was the 13th guest at the Lord's Supper.
- Jesus was crucified on a Friday.
- On Friday, October 13th, 1307, King Philip IV of France ordered the dismantling of the Knights Templar, leading to the torture and executions of hundreds of Knights.

The problem with "evidence" such as this is that it does not take into account tragedies that have happened on dates other that Friday the 13th, nor does it consider many of the positive associations with Friday and 13 throughout history and tradition. For example:

- In Israel, Friday the 13th is revered as an extraordinarily lucky day.
- In Judaism, the Sabbath begins Friday evening, the Bar Mitzvah is held at age 13, and there are 13 months in the Hebrew lunar calendar.

- A gold charm in the shape of the number 13 is given to Italian infants to ensure good luck and prosperity as they grow.
- There were 13 original colonies in America, 13 stars and stripes on the original American flag, and the 13th amendment freed the slaves.
- We owe Hershey's chocolate to a man born on Friday the 13th —Milton Hershey, and many movie buffs are grateful for the Friday the 13th birth of Alfred Hitchcock.

These lists demonstrate that it is as easy to stack evidence in favor of Friday the 13th as it is to stack the deck against it.

Looking at some of the ways to ward off the "bad luck" of the day may lend humor to the subject. For example, in France, a group of people who called themselves "fourteeners" used to offer themselves as dinner guests to remedy the bad luck of having a group of 13. Folklore recommends climbing to the top of a mountain and burning all your socks with holes in them, or standing on your head while eating a piece of gristle. Fortunately, today we have effective treatments for the phobia itself. And, for what it's worth, one 49-year-old woman was very grateful she did not stay home on Friday, February 13th, 2004, for that was the day she hit the $10.2 million jackpot at MGM Grand in Las Vegas.

Chapter 10

MORE ON SOCIAL PHOBIA

- What is social phobia?
- Why am I so afraid to speak in public?
- What can I do to help with my fear of public speaking?
- Can I take medicine to help my fear of public speaking?
- My daughter is isolating herself at school and won't answer questions in class. Her teacher thinks she has social phobia. What are the features of social phobia in children, and how can I help her?
- What is the difference between agoraphobia and social phobia?
- I have a lot of social fears. They started in high school with a dread of public speaking. Then I couldn't eat in public. From there, I couldn't use a public restroom, and more recently, I couldn't go to a party. I am getting quite worried. Is this unusual?
- I have seen ads on television that claim Zoloft can help with social phobia. How can a drug help me be more social?
- When I go to a party, I feel very uncomfortable and end up wishing I had just stayed home. How does this happen?
- How can I improve my problems with social phobia?
- What are some behaviors I can use to desensitize myself to social anxiety?

What is social phobia?

Some people develop an intense fear of embarrassing or humiliating themselves in public. Although they realize their concern may be excessive or even silly, their anxiety is still overwhelming. We call this **social phobia**, also known as social anxiety disorder. People with social phobia suffer in one or more social or performance situations, such as:

- Eating in public
- Writing checks in public
- Public speaking or stage fright (because these fears are so common, they are only diagnosed as social phobia when they lead to significant impairment or distress)
- Talking to a boss or other authority figure
- Dating (for more on dating anxiety, see chapter 15)
- Going to parties
- Using public restrooms

If you have social phobia, you may imagine that others are always looking at you and secretly mocking or criticizing you. You also tend to think that everyone else is competent in the situation and you are not. People with social phobia tend to overestimate how threatening or condemning others are and underestimate their own ability to cope with social situations. Still, individuals with social phobia may function quite well unless they are faced with doing the particularly feared public activity. At that time, they may suffer marked anticipatory anxiety as well as intense anxiety when actually faced with the dreaded social encounter. Fortunately, about 80% of people who undergo cognitive-behavioral treatment, some while taking prescription medication, find a great deal of relief.

Why am I so afraid to speak in public?

Keep in mind that public speaking is probably the number one fear among all people, so you are not alone. Approximately 40 to 60 million people share this fear with you.

When afraid of public speaking, people often have ideas in their mind like: "I'll make a fool of myself. I won't know what to say. People will think I'm stupid. I won't know how to answer their questions. I'll never live it down. It must be perfect. If I mess up, it would be awful." Obviously, this kind of self-talk makes you very self-conscious and nervous, and sets you up to notice any little mistake in what you say or do. Focusing on any perceived problems in your presentation makes you more nervous, and you have a vicious cycle in motion.

As far as figuring out how to make this problem better, first assess your motivation. What are the benefits of getting more comfortable with public speaking? What are the costs of doing so? Some people can happily go through life without ever having to speak in public. Others may feel they are missing out on opportunities or an important life experience if they avoid public speaking. If you want to speak in public, the next question covers techniques that can help you face your fear.

What can I do to help with my fear of public speaking?

Here are some ways to address your fear and mobilize yourself to speak publicly:

1. Challenge your self-talk. If you've prepared for a presentation, then telling yourself "I won't know what to say" really isn't true.

2. Question your own estimates of how dangerous or threatening you think the audience is:
   - Exactly how dangerous can the audience be to you?
   - What's the worst thing that could happen?
   - Even if you did make a mistake, how bad would that be?
   - Don't most people make some mistakes when they are giving speeches?

3. Recall speeches you've heard or meetings you've attended:
   - How much did you actually think about the speakers' performance after the talk was completed?
   - Did you go home and talk about it at dinner, think about it through your evening, tell friends about it the next day? Probably not.
   - Keep in mind that people are usually far more focused on themselves than they are on other people.

4. Expose yourself to public speaking situations. You can become an expert on effective self-talk, but if you never give yourself a chance to try it out, your fear of public speaking will probably remain. You might develop a list of possible tasks you could do to increase your comfort level with public speaking, such as making an announcement in a comfortable group setting or

practicing a speech with a close friend. Over time, you can work up to more difficult assignments.

5. Join an organization such as Toastmasters to help you practice your public speaking and grow more comfortable with it. Practice is key.

6. When you speak, bring notes with you to reduce your anxiety about forgetting what you are saying.

7. Talk with people who speak regularly and ask them about their experiences. Did they start out feeling so at ease with public speaking? Probably not, but with repeated exposures to giving presentations, they probably became more comfortable. Also ask whether they still feel some degree of anxiety or nervousness. They'll probably tell you yes.

Keep in mind that some anxiety can actually enhance performance—it's the adrenaline that makes you sharp and able to think on your feet. Tell yourself to turn the anxiety into excitement, and channel that energy into your speech! Also remind yourself, "No one can see on the outside what I'm feeling on the inside."

Can I take medicine to help my fear of public speaking?

There are a variety of medications that can ease the anxiety associated with social phobia. Individuals may find relief with benzodiazepines, SSRI and MAOI antidepressants, as well as with beta-blockers. Beta-blockers are often used for this type of social phobia. They take effect within a short period of time and are metabolized by the body quickly, so you can use them in preparation for a performance situation. Another advantage of these medications is that they don't cause dependency. Keep in mind that beta-blockers lower your blood pressure, so make sure you get this medication through a doctor who can assess and monitor you. Also, remember that although medications can help take the edge off during stressful situations, facing your fear is the best way to combat phobias.

My daughter is isolating herself at school and won't answer questions in class. Her teacher thinks she has social phobia. What are the features of social phobia in children, and how can I help her?

Children who suffer from social phobia have an intense fear of situations where they are expected to socialize or perform. As a result, they might experience a pounding heart, sweating, stomachaches, headaches, crying, and "freezing." Children with this problem dread having to start conversations with peers or talk in front of groups, two things that are usually essential for managing school adequately. So, socially anxious children might have a very difficult academic experience because they are unwilling to answer questions in class or make small talk to have friends. The Anxiety Disorders Association of America lists the following warning signs for social phobia:

- Discomfort and passivity when the child is the focus of attention
- Avoidance or refusal to start conversations, get together with friends, or call people on the phone
- Poor eye contact
- Soft, mumbled speech
- Limited interactions with peers
- Being on the edge of the social group and seeming withdrawn
- Discomfort with performing in front of others, such as answering a question in class
- Worry about being negatively evaluated, humiliated, or ridiculed by others

Be supportive, but also encourage your child to perform behaviors that will help reduce the anxiety. You can do this by participating in opportunities for her to be with other children, such as playgroups, church activities, going to the park, and attending birthday parties. It's also a good idea to help your daughter learn to speak up for herself—some examples include calling a friend, asking a store clerk where an item is, or ordering her own lunch.

If you are socially anxious, watch the messages that you send to your children. We teach by how we live, and if you demonstrate fearfulness and reluctance in social situations, your daughter may internalize beliefs that talking to others is too difficult or embarrassing. If you are struggling with your own social anxiety, this is a good time to get help for yourself. Our children often push us to address our limitations so that we can help them thrive.

Finally, as you and your daughter work together, notice and reward small steps, as this helps her build confidence, pride, and motivation to keep at it. Success in facing this fear will provide her a valuable experience to draw on throughout her life.

What's the difference between agoraphobia and social phobia?

People with agoraphobia are afraid of 1) leaving home, 2) being alone, and 3) being in situations where they may feel trapped, helpless, and unable to escape. These fears occur while using public transportation, being in crowds, attending public places (theaters, restaurants, supermarkets, and department stores), or waiting in line. People become so fearful of having a panic attack and feeling helpless that they avoid places where panic attacks might happen. Many individuals become housebound.

In contrast, individuals with social phobia are more concerned with normal public activities that may result in social criticism and humiliation than with the possibility of feeling trapped or helpless. Whereas individuals with social phobia can also suffer panic attacks, the anxiety associated with social phobia is likely to involve blushing, sweating and dry mouth. Individuals with social phobia may resist drawing attention to themselves or interacting with others, but they generally do not avoid public situations to the point that they are almost homebound.

I have a lot of social fears. They started in high school with a dread of public speaking. Then I couldn't eat in public. From there, I couldn't use a public restroom, and more recently, I couldn't go to a party. I am getting quite worried. Is this unusual?

You describe what we call **generalized social phobia**. This variant of social phobia is diagnosed when a person has a variety of social fears, including both performance and social interaction situations. The generalized phobia is a more serious and impairing condition than a specific social phobia. Usually it has an earlier age of onset, and the sufferers are more likely to be single and to have more pronounced fears about interaction with others. Unfortunately, it also is associated with clinical depression and alcoholism. Your concern is warranted, as such phobias can escalate until they are addressed in treatment. Start with an evaluation by a mental health professional with expertise in anxiety disorders. You may want a dual evaluation by a therapist who provides exposure therapy in conjunction with a psychiatrist who can evaluate whether medication might help you. Both cognitive-behavioral therapy and medications, such as SSRI antidepressants, benzodiazepines, and beta-blockers, have been found to be valuable in the treatment of social phobia.

I have seen ads on television that claim Zoloft can help with social phobia. How can a drug help me be more social?

If you have social phobia, you experience intense fears of being humiliated while doing normal activities in public. Public speaking is the most common. Other dreaded situations include signing documents in front of others, eating in public places, undergoing interviews, using public restrooms, and going to parties. The anxiety becomes a huge barrier to being social. The disorder can be chronic, distressing, and impairing.

Several medications can be very helpful, including SSRI antidepressants, of which Zoloft is one. These medications encourage a particular brain chemical called **serotonin**, which is associated with feelings of well-being, to stay present and active between nerve cells. Usually the body is not only making chemicals but also metabolizing them. SSRIs allow less serotonin to be broken down. As a result, the serotonin lasts longer and has more of an influence on nerve cells. Originally designed to treat clinical depression by improving mood, the SSRIs are effective in reducing anxiety symptoms as well. So if you are anxious about usual public activities and you are treated with an SSRI, your reduced anxiety level may permit you to be more social.

When I go to a party, I feel very uncomfortable and end up wishing I had just stayed home. How does this happen?

If you trace the sequence of your thoughts, feelings and behaviors from your anticipation of the party to your conclusion that you can't handle it, you will see how each step feeds the next, causing your anxiety to escalate. Here's an example:

Social Phobia Sequence

Thoughts: "I don't want to go to this party. I won't have a good time."

Feelings/Sensations: Anxious, tense, nervous
Tightness in neck, shoulders, or stomach
Increasing heart rate

Behavior: Stumbles as she is walking up the stairs to the party, drops purse and spills its contents

Thoughts: "I'm such an idiot. I've already made a fool of myself."
Feelings/Sensations: Anxious, tense, nervous, embarrassed, mad
More tightness in neck/shoulders.
Nausea
Faster heart rate, beginning to sweat

Behavior: Gets a drink and withdraws into a corner, doesn't initiate conversation with anyone

Thoughts: "Nobody even looks at me; nobody cares if I'm here. They know I don't have anything interesting to say."

Feelings/Sensations: Anxious, tense, nervous, embarrassed, mad
Continued tightness in neck/shoulders
Nausea
Heart racing, sweating
Hands shaking

Behavior: Spills some of her drink when someone accidentally bumps into her, apologizes repeatedly

Thoughts: "I sound so stupid. I knew I shouldn't have come. I've got to get out of here."

Behavior: Quietly sneaks out of the party without saying anything to anyone

Feelings/Sensations: Less anxious, tense
Physical symptoms decrease
RELIEF

Thoughts: "Thank God I got out of there. I'm never going to another party again."

Result: Avoidance gets reinforced because of *temporary* relief, but long-term problems with anxiety are maintained.

How can I improve my problems with social phobia?

People with social phobia overestimate how harshly they will be judged and underestimate their ability to cope. More realistic thoughts about the degree of others' scrutiny, as well as acknowledgment of your strengths, are important in challenging social phobia. It's a good idea to remember that people are usually far more

Anxious Self-Talk	More Realistic Self-Talk
I won't know what to say.	I can figure out something to say.
They'll think I'm a loser.	I can't read their mind and I don't control what they think. I'll just do my best.
I always get nervous and act like a fool.	It's okay to be a little nervous. My friends say I act fine. Calling myself a fool doesn't help me.
I shouldn't feel this anxious—people are going to laugh at me.	I feel how I feel, and nobody can see on the outside what I'm feeling inside.
I've always been a shy person—I'll never get over this.	Just because I'm shy doesn't mean I can't learn to be more comfortable talking in groups.
It's awful to be rejected.	Rejection is a part of life and happens to everyone at some point. Being rejected is inconvenient, but I could survive it.
If I don't make a good first impression, I won't get the job.	I can't control how others perceive me, but I'll do my best. If I don't get the job, I'll be disappointed, but it won't be the end of the world.
I'm too dull for anyone to ever ask me out.	I have many interests and calling myself dull makes me feel bad. People aren't dull; only conversations can be dull.
I can't stand making mistakes in front of other people. It will be horrible if I can't answer all these questions.	Nobody likes making mistakes, but I can stand it if I do. There's no reason I must be able to answer all their questions. If I don't know the answer, I'll tell them that I'll find out and get back to them.

focused on themselves and their lives than on you. To demonstrate this, try writing a list of all the topics someone could be thinking or talking about *besides* you.

More important, practice changing the way you talk to yourself about social situations. Below are some examples to transform anxiety-producing self-talk into more realistic and calming self-talk:

What are some behaviors I can use to desensitize myself to social anxiety?

The behaviors in the chart on the next page are great ways to face situations you fear. Albert Ellis referred to many of these actions as "shame-attacking" exercises. By completing a perceived risky behavior, you show yourself that you can stand the things you thought you couldn't stand. You begin to liberate yourself from constant worries about how others are judging you. If an idea sounds strange, that's okay. Think how pleasantly surprised you'll be when you find out you can do it!

Finally, if you dread and resist "small talk," challenge yourself to see its value. We live in a social world and small talk is a part of life— in academic, professional, and social settings. You can generate and practice possible topics of conversation to improve your comfort level. Many people benefit from asking a friend to role-play with them so they can practice starting and maintaining conversations. Asking people about their experiences and finding aspects to which you can relate are usually good strategies.

Accept a compliment

Give a compliment

Go out of your way to speak to three people you hardly know at work each day

Make an announcement during a PTA meeting

Make an announcement during the church service

Eat alone in a crowded restaurant

Offer to write something on the board in a work meeting

Volunteer to call participants for a meeting

Drink in front of others

Send out an email with deliberate mistakes

Drop a glass of water on purpose in a restaurant

Begin a new hobby where you are likely to make mistakes

Raise your hand to ask a question in class

Volunteer to give a toast at a wedding

Deliberately take longer to pay for an item at the store

Ask for an item that the store definitely does not carry

Ask 5 people out on dates with the goal of being rejected

Post a memo with at least one typo

Call out each floor while you're riding on the elevator

Carry a large black umbrella when it's really hot and clear outside

Wear one black shoe and one brown one to school or work

Chapter 11

UNDERSTANDING OBSESSIVE-COMPULSIVE DISORDER

■ What is obsessive-compulsive disorder, and how is it related to my anxiety?

■ I check things all the time—my locks, my stove, the iron. I know I don't need to, but I feel like I have to. What is my problem?

■ How common is OCD, and what is its typical course?

■ Does having OCD mean there is something really wrong with my brain?

■ What is the difference between obsessions and compulsions?

■ What are some examples of obsessions?

■ What are examples of compulsions?

■ How are obsessions and compulsions connected?

■ What's the difference between an obsessive-compulsive personality disorder and an obsessive-compulsive disorder?

■ How can OCD affect families?

■ I have OCD and feel terrible about myself. How are the two related?

■ What are rituals, and what makes them healthy or unhealthy?

■ I'm a good organizer, and I like to keep things in order. Does that mean I'm compulsive?

■ I can't seem to send an email or write a letter without checking it over numerous times. Does this mean I have OCD?

■ Some of my friends have said my 9-year-old son has OCD. How do I know if this is true?

■ I'm kind of picky, and my friends say I'm "anal." Where did that reference come from, and what does it mean?

■ I think of my gambling as an addiction, but we call it "compulsive gambling." Are addictions the same as compulsions?

What is obsessive-compulsive disorder, and how is it related to my anxiety?

Obsessive-compulsive disorder, or OCD, is an anxiety disorder in which the sufferer experiences recurring **obsessions** (intrusive, anxiety-provoking thoughts, impulses or images) and/or **compulsions** (behaviors or mental acts aimed at reducing anxiety that but actually intensify the problem). Obsessions and compulsions feed each other and ultimately make anxiety worse. Obsessions create anxiety, and compulsions attempt to reduce that anxiety, but only do so temporarily. Obsessions come back more strongly, compulsions are repeated and expanded, and so on. The following chart shows how thoughts, feelings and behaviors flow into one another and maintain OCD symptoms:

Obsessions
Intrusive thoughts or images regarding
contamination, morality, sexuality, danger

➤

Distress
Anxiety, shame, disgust

➤

Compulsions
Repetitive behaviors or mental acts to lessen
distress from obsessions

➤

Temporary relief

➤

Obsessions
Intrusive thoughts or images regarding
contamination, morality, sexuality, danger

➤

Distress
Anxiety, shame, disgust
➡
Compulsions
Repetitive behaviors or mental acts to
lessen distress from obsessions
➡
Temporary relief
➡
...and on and on
➡
Long-standing distress

I check things all the time—my locks, my stove, the iron. I know I don't need to, but I feel like I have to. What is my problem?

If you are engaging in these types of behaviors repeatedly, up to more than one hour a day, you might be suffering from what we call **obsessive-compulsive disorder**, or **OCD**. Excessive checking may constitute a compulsion—the tendency to engage in repeated, unwelcome behaviors. People diagnosed with OCD suffer from disturbing thoughts/images and compulsions (which can be overt behaviors or mental rituals). If your checking behaviors are indeed compulsions, here are two important criteria a trained professional will look for before applying the OCD diagnosis:

1. You are aware, at least at some point, that the obsessions or compulsions you experience are excessive or unreasonable.
2. The obsessions or compulsions (a) are extremely distressing, (b) take up more than an hour of your day, or (c) interfere significantly with your usual way of living.

Obviously, a self-help book cannot diagnose you. If your checking behaviors are causing you distress or disrupting your life, consult with a trained professional for a diagnostic assessment and recommendations for treatment.

How common is OCD, and what is its typical course?

According to the National Institute of Mental Health, the lifetime prevalence for OCD is about 2.3%. In other words, OCD occurs in about one in every 43 people at some point in their lives. Due to the reluctance of OCD sufferers to admit their symptoms, the figures we have are likely to be lower than the actual rates. However, this is changing as people learn more about the disorder, and researchers have found significant increases in prevalence rates compared to earlier studies.

The onset of the disorder usually is in late adolescence or the early twenties, but it can also begin in childhood. The start of OCD is typically fairly gradual. Men and women tend to show similar rates of OCD, but women might be more likely to seek treatment. OCD is a chronic illness, with waxing and waning symptoms that can be worsened by stress and hormonal changes. People may suffer for years before seeking treatment—often with significant impairments in their school, work, social, and family functioning. OCD can be particularly hard on marriages—one spouse might feel consumed with performing compulsions as a primary life focus, while the other spouse might feel confused and helpless. Individuals with OCD might also struggle with depression, sleep problems, excessive worry, social anxiety, specific phobias, and panic attacks. Relationships between OCD and eating disorders, and OCD and Tourette's Syndrome (a tic disorder) have also been identified. Given the toll that OCD can take on a person, the earlier the diagnosis and initiation of treatment, the better.

In studies comparing the rates of various compulsions, checking and cleaning were the most common, followed in descending order by: counting, needing to ask or confess, symmetry/ordering rituals, and hoarding. The majority of people with OCD have numerous obsessions, and about half of OCD sufferers report having multiple compulsive rituals. Notably, the nature of obsessions and compulsions can change over time.

Does having OCD mean there is something really wrong with my brain?

OCD is considered to be a neurobehavioral condition. The following findings provide evidence that the brains of people with OCD are different than the brains of people who don't have OCD:

- Brain scans show overactivity in the basal ganglia, caudate nucleus, and the orbital frontal regions of OCD brains compared with non-OCD brains.
- Inadequate levels of serotonin have been implicated in OCD— numerous studies have shown that OCD symptoms decline in response to medications (SSRIs) that keep more serotonin available in the brain. The strong biological contribution in OCD is further revealed by the fact that there is an increased risk of having OCD if your parents have it.

In general, OCD brains have a hard time saying "Enough—I don't need to run this through again." Instead, an OCD brain says, "Do it again—more, more, more." Experts in the area have referred to OCD as "brain lock" (Schwartz), a "brain traffic jam," a "brain hiccup" (Rappaport), and "brain junk mail" (Chansky), to name a few. Repetitions of thoughts and behaviors occur because the mind has imposed a demand for a guarantee. Underlying basically all OCD thoughts and behaviors is the idea that "I have to be sure."

Unfortunately for people guided by this message, life does not provide complete certainty or guarantees.

The good news is that successful treatment with either cognitive-behavioral therapy or medications has been shown to diminish the OCD brain overactivity and to increase levels of serotonin. People with OCD can gain control over their symptoms and improve their quality of life.

What is the difference between obsessions and compulsions?

Obsessions are thoughts, and compulsions are behaviors. Here are the definitions of the terms:

Obsessions are *thoughts, impulses or mental images* that happen without your wanting them to and cause you stress. People who meet criteria for OCD tend to have these unwelcome mental thoughts or images for at least one hour a day. Some examples of obsessions might be wondering if your hands are clean or thinking someone else's hands weren't clean enough for you to have shaken. Obsessions can also involve thinking you left the stove turned on and that it could start a fire. Some people with OCD experience recurring, intrusive, and unwanted images of violent or sexual acts.

Compulsions are unwelcome, repetitive *behaviors* such as washing your hands repeatedly, putting things in a certain order, hoarding your belongings and not being able to throw things away, making sure a door is locked, checking a stove to be sure it is turned off, or repeatedly vacuuming the carpet. In general, people who do compulsions recognize that their behaviors are excessive and unreasonable, but they think they can't stand it if they don't do these actions.

What are some examples of obsessions?

Obsessions generally involve an exaggerated sense of personal responsibility and a need for certainty. Here is a list of obsession categories and examples:

Harm

That candle might start a fire.

A burglar might harm me while I'm sleeping.

I could drop my baby while walking down these stairs.

(While driving) Did I just run over someone?

Contamination

I touched the door handle—it has all kinds of germs that will make me sick.

I better not shake her hand—I could contract AIDS.

I can't sit on the floor—it's filthy. I'll get sick and die.

Did that waitress touch my hamburger?

Certainty

Did I lock the door?

Is the iron turned off?

Did I forget to put a stamp on that envelope I mailed?

Did I say goodbye to her before walking away?

Order

It feels wrong if the towels aren't lined up exactly.

I can't stand it if the comforter is wrinkled.

To do my homework, I need three pencils lined up perfectly.

I can't watch television if the pictures on the wall aren't completely straight.

Numbers
I need to check the door handle 21 times before I can be sure it's
   locked.
I have to brush my teeth for 45 seconds—no more, no less.
The light is off after I have flicked the switch 12 times.
I have to say this prayer 10 times before I can go to sleep.

Religiosity/Scrupulosity
Having that thought means I'm a bad person.
Something will happen to my family if I don't pray hard enough.
I'm afraid I will steal things.
The teacher must punish kids who tease others.

Hoarding
I have to keep this trash—something important might have gotten
   thrown away.
I can't throw out these magazines and newspapers—I might need
   them later.
The more papers I have, the better.
I can't get rid of any of my children's old schoolwork—it's too
   important.

Sexual Thoughts/Images
I had a dream about another man—I must be gay.
I can't help picturing my boss without any clothes on—I'm terrible.
If I accidentally touch my chest, I am sinful.

What are examples of compulsions?

Compulsions are repetitive behaviors or mental acts that decrease anxiety in the short-term, but lead to an increasingly strong desire to do the compulsion over the long-term. In this way, compulsions feed themselves and become less effective over time, requiring more energy or elaboration. Here are some common categories and examples:

Washing and cleaning: vacuuming after anyone enters the room, repeated hand-washing

Checking: stopping the car repeatedly to see if someone was run over, checking locks repeatedly

Keeping things in order: lining up items in the cupboard in alphabetical order, hanging clothes in exactly the same spot every day

Counting: counting the number of cracks in the sidewalk or the number of billboards along the road

Repeating/Redoing: rewriting a casual note 25 times until it is "just right," balancing the checkbook over and over to make sure you did it right

Hoarding: saving useless items, inspecting the trash to make sure nobody threw out anything "valuable"

Praying: saying a prayer over and over in order to keep bad thoughts away

How are obsessions and compulsions connected?

Above we discussed the difference between obsessions and compulsions. Here's an example of how the two are related. First, obsessive thoughts begin: "I can't stand it if the floor is dirty." "Is the floor dirty?" "Is there dirt on the floor?" "Did somebody walk on the floor?" Those repeated unwelcome thoughts cause distress in the form of anger, panic, or anxiety. In order to relieve that distress a person does what is called a compulsion. In the example described, if I think I can't stand dirt on the floor and I feel distressed by this thought, then I vacuum the floor—a compulsion. I do the compulsion to relieve the anxiety created by the obsessive thought. Interestingly, once I vacuum the floor, I do feel better. I'm relieved at least for the short-term. However, the next time somebody walks on the floor or it looks like somebody spilled something, my anxiety builds up again because I start having the negative thoughts: "Oh no, is the carpet dirty?" "What's in there?" "I'd better clean it up." Obsessions are the thoughts that produce distress. Compulsions are the behaviors performed repeatedly to relieve the distress. The problem is the relief is only short-term. By doing the compulsions, the person keeps him or herself in a long-standing cycle of distress.

What's the difference between an obsessive-compulsive personality disorder and an obsessive-compulsive disorder?

Many people are puzzled about the difference between obsessive-compulsive disorder (OCD) and obsessive-compulsive personality disorder (OCPD). First of all, OCD is categorized as an anxiety disorder, whereas OCPD is one of the personality disorders. Although an anxiety disorder is experienced as very distressing, a personality disorder is not necessarily troublesome to the person who has it. Personality disorders refer to patterns of thinking, feeling, and relating that deviate significantly from the expectations of the person's culture. In other words, the people who live and work with someone with a personality disorder may be the ones who are distressed. People with OCPD tend to relate to the world in some of the following ways:

- They tend to be perfectionistic, which interferes with task completion.
- They are very focused on rules, details, and order, to the extent that they lose sight of the point of the activity.
- They want control over the way things are done, and because of this, have difficulty delegating responsibility.
- They value work and productivity over leisure activities and friendships.
- They are rigid and inflexible about matters of morality and ethics.
- They assume that if others were more like them, the world would be a better place.

In addition, OCD develops more like an illness, and includes a pattern of distressing, unwelcome, repetitive thoughts and behaviors; OCPD is a long-standing and ingrained way of responding to people and situations.

How can OCD affect families?

Witnessing the anxious and repetitive behaviors of a family member with OCD can be frustrating, and can lead to power struggles and conflict. Although persistent family conflict is not enough to cause OCD, it can make symptoms worse. It's best when family members can unite and work together against OCD, rather than family members working against the *person* diagnosed with OCD. Coping with OCD in the family can be very challenging, but frequent arguing, yelling, and blaming of the patient tend to make things worse. If you are the loved one of an individual suffering from OCD, keep in mind that the affected family member did not choose to have OCD—it is a neuropsychiatric condition with an involuntary nature. Keep in mind:

- Your partner does not wash his hands 75+ times per day, to the point that they are red and raw, for the purposes of annoying you or getting attention—he does it to relieve the distress associated with thinking that his hands are dirty and something bad will happen as a result.
- Your child does not repeatedly walk over to check the stove setting just to get on your nerves—she does it because OCD makes her believe "I have to be sure the stove is off, and I'm not sure—what if a fire starts because the stove was left on?"
- No matter how bizarre, compulsive behaviors or rituals are performed to neutralize obsessive thoughts and decrease feelings of distress.

Understanding how OCD works is a great tool for family members to keep their negative emotions from becoming extreme. Remember that OCD fears are very real to the person suffering from them. Being a collaborator in the patient's treatment is extremely beneficial. Family members who appreciate "OCD tricks" are great coaches with helping distinguish "Jenny's thoughts" from "OCD thoughts." Further, family members can be excellent motivators for doing gradual, effective exposure with response prevention. Obviously, you don't want to push your daughter into facing an OCD fear that feels too overwhelming at the time, but you also don't want to promote her avoidance of her fears such that OCD gets more of a hold on her life.

I have OCD and feel terrible about myself. How are the two related?

Remember that you are suffering from a neuropsychiatric disorder that comes with certain ways of thinking. Here are some characteristics of OCD that can drain anyone's self-concept:

1. **Self-doubt** is a hallmark of OCD. Your OCD makes it difficult for you to trust your perceptions. So you check, still don't trust your checking, and then check again. It is hard to feel confident when you are always second-guessing yourself.

2. **Feeling responsible** is also a feature of OCD. The OCD version of responsibility, however, extends beyond *your* behaviors, and includes events over which you have no actual control. For example, you believe you can cause negative events by thinking negative thoughts. In addition, you obsess about decisions out of a belief that you are *supposed* to know every possible outcome and make the perfect decision. If anything does go wrong, it is your fault.

3. **Guilt** goes hand-in-hand with the excessive feelings of responsibility. Just having a passing negative thought can feel like committing a crime.

So when you think of what you're up against—the expectation to be completely responsible while at the same time doubting every turn you take—it is understandable that you feel bad about yourself. You have made a huge first step, which is to acknowledge that you have this disorder. The next step is to become clear that this disorder is not YOU. Through treatment, you can learn to distinguish your thoughts and behaviors from those "mandated" by OCD.

What are rituals, and what makes them healthy or unhealthy?

A ritual is a repeated behavior. Rituals can be performed individually or in the context of a community or religious group. Humans are naturally drawn to social rituals—from the wedding ceremony to the goodbye kiss—as a way of marking important events and transitions. Such rituals can provide a sense of bonding among members of a family or community and help honor important life passages. Religious rituals can provide a break in the routines of life to allow reflection and higher awareness. Individuals also naturally develop rituals to ease transitions and organize their days—from the morning cup of coffee to prayers at bedtime.

Determining whether a ritual is healthy or unhealthy depends on how the performance of the ritual makes you feel and the reason behind the ritual. If you repeat a behavior because you want to do it, you feel good when you do it, and it has good consequences, then the ritual would seem healthy. The following indicators suggest that a ritual may not be healthy:

- You repeatedly perform a behavior out of fear and to prevent something bad from happening. For example, you believe that if you don't kiss your son on both cheeks before he leaves for school, something terrible will happen to him.

- The ritual is time-consuming and occupies more of the day than you'd like. For example, you have so many rituals before a meal that your food gets cold before you eat it.
- Doing the ritual leads to increased performance of the ritual and gets you in a vicious cycle.

It may be helpful to look at the example of prayer. Some people pray because they are afraid that if they don't something bad will happen to one of their family members. They may be praying hundreds of times during the day: each time they cross the street, leave the house, answer the phone, etc. These kinds of rituals, which are clearly motivated out of fear, are obviously distressing. They produce only short-term relief and perpetuate long-term pain.

On the other hand, people who pray repeatedly throughout the day because it gives them joy, helps them feel closer to God, and lifts their spirit would probably consider prayer to be a healthy ritual for them. While the behaviors in these two examples are similar, it is the reason for the ritual that determines whether it is distressing or healthy.

I'm a good organizer, and I like to keep things in order. Does that mean I'm compulsive?

There is a difference between being a *good* organizer and being a *compulsive* organizer. Good organizers have skills at managing large amounts of information, a busy calendar, and even people. Organizing is most helpful when it makes things run more smoothly and efficiently. For example, by filing your papers under separate categories, you will be able to get the document you need easily and quickly. If you leave them in a big pile, you will have to rummage through that pile every time you need something. Sometimes creating order can help us feel more calm and in control of our lives.

These benefits are outweighed by difficulties when organizing takes on the qualities of a compulsion. The behaviors associated with a compulsion are repetitive and excessive, and are more directed at neutralizing fears than at making life easier. Consider, for example, the organizational skills of someone who successfully gets her children to school and soccer practice, runs a growing business, volunteers, and hosts a book club. Now compare this to someone who spends hours inside her house, counting her pairs of socks and arranging (and rearranging) them in a particular order in her drawer. In the first case, the woman's life is wide and rich due to her ability to organize her time and schedule. In the second case, the woman's life is narrow and limited due to her compulsive need to organize. Although she may experience temporary relief through compulsive activity, she is also likely to feel trapped and distressed by her behavior.

If you enjoy organizing and are good at it, this is not a problem and there is no reason to call yourself "compulsive." When we hear of a label or diagnosis like this, it is easy to worry that it applies to us. The reality is that we all have a little bit of any diagnosis in us. It is a common phenomenon for psychiatry residents or psychology graduate students to be convinced they have many diagnoses they study. Be careful not to over-diagnose yourself. However, if a certain problem takes over and makes life difficult, obtaining a professional diagnosis may be essential to get the help you need.

I can't seem to send an email or write a letter without checking it over numerous times. Does this mean I have OCD?

Repeatedly checking emails or other letters can be a symptom of obsessive-compulsive disorder, but it doesn't have to be. The question to ask yourself is, "How distressing is this behavior?" Let's say you check your email five times before you send it, taking up 2–3 minutes of your time. If you then send it and don't think about it anymore, this behavior is probably not a sign of OCD. If, however, you spend a grueling hour reading over the same email and it feels like you can't stop this might be a significant behavior of which to take note. Think about what you are telling yourself when you repeatedly go over your email or your letter. Are you saying "I can't send this unless it's perfect"? Are you saying "It would be terrible if someone saw a mistake in what I've written"? If you think it would be awful if your email has a mistake or isn't perfect, then these thoughts are likely to make you feel anxious and result in your checking and rechecking what you've written. A good thing to do is to question your self-talk. How bad would it really be if you sent an email with a mistake in it? You may prefer not to do that and it may be inconvenient, but it certainly wouldn't be the end of the world. In fact, a common therapy assignment is to purposely make mistakes and send off their letters so they can see "I can stand mailing this off, even if it has a mistake and isn't perfect. It's not the end of the world."

Some of my friends have said my 9-year-old son has OCD. How do I know if this is true?

It is important to distinguish OCD behavior from typical habits of childhood and sometime the two can be confusing. The following chart contrasts OCD behaviors with typical childhood behaviors (Chansky, 2000):

OCD behaviors	Typical childhood habits
Take a great deal of time	Don't consume much time
Disrupt the typical routine	Don't disrupt the day's routine
Result in stress or frustration	May be enjoyable or pleasurable
Seem strange or unusual	Seem relatively ordinary
Intensify over time	Decrease in importance over time
Must be carried out in an exact way to avoid negative outcomes	Can be altered or forgotten without anything bad happening

To illustrate the difference, let's look at an example of a child brushing his teeth repeatedly. This behavior fits with OCD if the child feels he has to brush his teeth eight times in a row or his dad might be in a car accident. If, on the other hand, the child has told you he likes the way his new toothpaste tastes and he likes the fun container that it's in, and brushes his teeth five, six, seven times throughout the day, he's probably just doing it because it's fun.

I'm kind of picky, and my friends say I'm "anal." Where did that reference come from, and what does it mean?

The word "anal" may seem a strange way of describing someone's personality, but it has a basis in theory. The term comes out of psychoanalysis and its theories of personality development, dating back to thinkers such as Sigmund Freud. Freud believed that our personalities develop in stages, each under the influence of a body zone that provided intense pleasure. The three body zones observed were the oral, anal, and genital areas. The theory was that, if the needs of that stage were not adequately met, the growing child could become *fixated* at the stage associated with a certain body zone. So if the baby becomes fixated at the first stage (oral—birth to age one), she may later exhibit an "oral personality." Signs of this fixation theoretically include behaviors such as overeating, cigarette smoking and use of drugs or alcohol.

The "anal zone," which is midway between the oral and genital zones, is the focus of ages one to three. According to psychoanalytic theory, the toddler at this stage has come to enjoy opening his anal sphincter at any moment the impulse arises. At least in industrialized societies, it is considered important to save this activity for the proper place—a toilet. As the toddler gains voluntary control over defecation, he is faced with the dilemma, "Do I please my parents or myself?" The parental requirement of control conflicts with the pleasure of spontaneity. No other bodily muscle is the source of such a struggle. If a child wants to be oppositional, he can refuse to use the toilet, becoming what psychoanalysts call anal-explosive or anal-sadistic.

The child can, however, move in the other direction and become anal-retentive. This is usually what people are referring to when they say someone is "anal." With an emphasis on control and (resentfully) accommodating her parents, the growing child becomes overcontrolling on all matters. She collects and hoards many objects, and may hold onto her emotions as well. Her high standard for proper defecation is applied to other elements of life, such as work, money, and moral restraints. The bottom line is that her personality functions like her sphincter, holding on to everything. Someone with an anal personality is likely to be orderly, punctual, and frugal, and may make a good worker for these reasons. On the other hand, the same person may alienate others by being stubborn, withholding, and judgmental.

Although there isn't solid research to back up the connection between the body zones and personality, the popular culture has found a place for the anal personality.

I think of my gambling as an addiction, but we call it "compulsive gambling." Are addictions the same as compulsions?

Compulsions and addictions are similar in that there is a repetitive nature to both, and both are done to relieve some sense of distress—*temporarily*. Albert Ellis has talked about a concept called **low frustration tolerance**. This is also known as "I can't stand it-itis." With both compulsions and addictions, there is an aspect of people thinking "I can't stand it if I don't…(vacuum the floor again, make another bet, have a cigarette)". The assumption that you can't stand it if you don't perform a certain behavior is faulty, and people benefit from challenging this belief. However, in the moment, the idea that you can't stand it without the substance or the behavior is really powerful. In all compulsions and most addictions, if you truly couldn't stand something, you would die, and that is not the case. Being able to tell yourself "I don't like how this feels, but I can stand it" is often the key factor in resisting performing a compulsion or in resisting using a drug or taking a drink.

Some experts have made the distinction that engaging in an addiction usually feels good and rewarding, whereas performing a compulsion can be quite distressing. People with OCD are bothered by the irrational nature of their behavior even as they feel compelled to do it. Addictions are more likely to be associated with denial. Finally, while addictions can be psychological—in that your self-talk is mostly saying you have to have the substance or behavior, they can also be physiological. For example, with drug use your body gets to a point where it craves a particular drug and you might go through withdrawal symptoms (shaking, headaches, nausea) if you don't have the particular drug in your system. Physiological addictions, which can also lead to dependence, may require more and more of the substance over time to keep you satisfied.

In the case of both addictions and compulsions, it is extremely helpful to have support for changing your behaviors. Having a sponsor to call when you feel you need a drink or a friend to get you out of the house when you are tempted to compulsively clean can be a great help. A therapist or treatment program can provide strategies and resources for resisting the compulsion or addiction. In the case of severe chemical addictions, which are distinguished from compulsions by physiological withdrawal symptoms, it may be necessary to be in a protective environment as you allow the chemical to leave your system.

Chapter 12

TREATING OBSESSIVE-COMPULSIVE DISORDER

- What is the preferred treatment for OCD?
- Can medicine help me with OCD?
- How does therapy help with OCD?
- Is there a cure for OCD?
- I don't feel ready to give up my compulsions completely. Is there a way for me to gradually give them up?
- My daughter suffers from obsessive-compulsive disorder. How can I help her?
- I frequently have scary thoughts that I have to try to get out of my head. Sometimes this works, but other times it doesn't. My family thinks I should get professional help—should I?
- I worry that saying certain words aloud will hurt my family. My therapist says that these are OCD thoughts and not *my* thoughts. How do I convince myself of that?
- I don't understand how making myself think my scary thoughts will help me. Can you explain this?

What is the preferred treatment for OCD?

Experts generally recommend cognitive-behavioral therapy alone or in combination with certain medications—an SSRI antidepressant or the tricyclic antidepressant clomipramine—as the initial intervention. Whether to use the combination of both medication and CBT as a first-line treatment depends on the severity of the OCD and the age of the patient. For younger patients and for people with mild OCD symptoms, it is recommended that CBT be tried alone at first. However, experts generally rate combination treatment (both CBT and medication) as the most beneficial treatment approach for most patients. If medications are successful in reducing acute OCD symptoms, then staying on the medication for an extended period of time (e.g., 1–2 years) becomes important also. It's not a good idea to take the medication for only a couple of months and stop. Further, for people who have repeatedly gotten better from OCD and then relapsed (i.e., the symptoms returned) over the course of years, life-long medication maintenance is often recommended.

Can medicine help me with OCD?

SSRI antidepressants can be helpful with OCD. Depending on the study, 35–60% of patients taking an SSRI experienced clinically significant improvements in their OCD symptoms. Whereas these gains are important in patients' lives, they often are not sufficient to eliminate the need for other types of treatment.

Probably the best approach for dealing with OCD is a therapy technique called **exposure with response prevention**, discussed elsewhere in this chapter. If someone's OCD symptoms are so severe that they will not tolerate the exposure with response prevention, then a mental health professional may decide the use of a benzodiazepine is warranted. Even in these cases, however, the medication should only be used temporarily, then tapered off over time. This approach allows the patient to calm down enough to tolerate the treatment, but guards against the risk of psychological and physical dependence associated with benzodiazepine use. Ultimately, it is better for patients to be able to learn that they can tolerate uncomfortable thoughts, feelings and behaviors and give themselves credit for this, rather than to give the medication the credit.

How does therapy help with OCD?

For OCD, the most important aspect of cognitive-behavioral therapy is called **exposure with response prevention (E/RP).** In this intervention, patients are encouraged to tolerate the distress associated with their obsessive thought without performing any ritual to decrease the distress (e.g., get hands dirty and not wash them, say bad words without saying a prayer of forgiveness). With repeated practice, E/RP results in the patient becoming desensitized to the obsessive fear. The patient learns he can stand to have the disturbing thought without "being imprisoned" by having to repeat certain behaviors to neutralize the negative thought. CBT also helps patients challenge the importance of their thoughts and dispute their "need" for certainty, sense of over-responsibility, and exaggerated estimates of danger.

For example, a person who washes his hands 75 times per day might do so to relieve the anxious feelings derived from the thought "I can't stand to have germs on my hands—I could get sick and die!" Each time this man washes his hands, he does feel better, temporarily, until the obsessive thought occurs again. To help this individual, E/RP therapy would actually have the person get his hands dirty and then not wash them. Obviously, this would produce anxious arousal. The patient would feel very uncomfortable at first. However, this arousal would decline over time, particularly with repeated soiling and no-washing behaviors. Other examples of exposure with response prevention include: buying something and throwing it away, turning the lights on or plugging in the curling iron before leaving the house, and deliberately making mistakes on Christmas cards. By doing each of these behaviors, people learn that they can tolerate anxiety and that it declines as they confront, rather than avoid, their fears. This process, which is represented by the graph below, is called desensitization or habituation, and it is one of the most predictable psychological responses known.

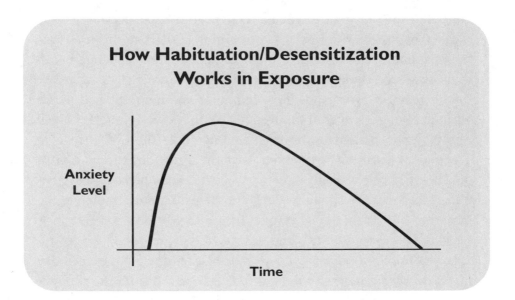

Is there a cure for OCD?

We wish there were a cure for OCD. However, as with most psychological disorders, it is better to think about "managing or coping with" OCD rather than "curing" it. Getting OCD under control is hard work, and it requires time and energy. The more people can accept this reality, the more they can focus on improving their quality of life. Taking an active role in reducing the symptoms of OCD, no matter how much you wish you didn't have to, is extremely important with OCD. Keep in mind that successful cognitive-behavioral psychotherapy and/or effective medication management can produce positive changes in OCD brains so that they look more similar to non-OCD brains on scans. Whereas eliminating all intrusive thoughts is impossible, realistic goals for managing OCD include:

1. Decreasing the frequency of and level of disturbance associated with obsessions
2. Stopping compulsive behaviors and ritualistic mental acts
3. Improving functioning in important areas of life
4. Developing tools to prevent the relapse of symptoms

I don't feel ready to give up my compulsions completely. Is there a way for me to gradually give them up?

Yes; small steps, such as delaying and altering rituals, can go a long way in helping you take charge of your OCD. Here are some helpful and creative strategies suggested by Edna Foa and Reid Wilson:

1. **Postpone your ritual:** Start to drive a wedge between you and the compulsion by waiting as long as you can to perform it. Even if you can only wait 30 seconds, that's a start! Then see if you can postpone it again. This strategy helps you begin to

take control of your compulsion, while learning to tolerate the distress you usually act on.

2. **Slow it down:** Do your ritual in slow motion. This is particularly effective with checking rituals. Because anxiety can make you feel pressured and frantic, slowing it down takes some of the power away from the experience. Also, going in slow motion helps you remember doing it, so you don't have to question yourself or repeat the ritual. Quick relaxation techniques, like taking a slow, calming breath, can help.

3. **Change your ritual.** Start by writing down the steps to your ritual as if you are instructing someone else to do it. List every detail, in the order they are supposed to occur. It will become apparent that you can make many small changes to your ritual. By doing so, you begin to bring this seemingly automatic response under your voluntary control.

My daughter suffers from obsessive-compulsive disorder. How can I help her?

If your child has been diagnosed with OCD, one of the best things you can do is understand the disorder and its clever deceit. An excellent resource to promote your understanding and provide you with tools to assist your child is Tamar Chansky's *Freeing Your Child from Obsessive-Compulsive Disorder.* Keep in mind the following:

1. Help your child understand there is a difference between OCD lies and the child's own thoughts: "Just because you *think* it doesn't make it true. You don't have to listen to that OCD trick. OCD feelings and directions are not facts—they try to mislead you."

2. Understand the short-term gain/long-term pain tradeoff. The more the child performs the compulsion to get relief from an

obsession, the more she has to keep doing the compulsion. It is important to realize that *the anxiety will pass whether the child does the compulsion or not.* Resisting doing the compulsion is one of the best ways for the child to learn that OCD lies and empower herself against this disorder. Tell your daughter that, while she does not control her OCD thoughts, she can control her behavior.

3. Be sensitive to the fact that OCD tries to insist that your child establish certainty in an uncertain world. Imagine what it's like to have your brain constantly telling you "But I have to be sure." Being sure all the time is impossible and the attempt to achieve this goal is exhausting. Help your child realize that "maybes" and "less than 100% certain" are manageable and healthier when fighting OCD. For the pervasive doubt that OCD uses as a weapon, Chansky recommended the following questions to help children distinguish OCD tricks from their own ideas:

It's an OCD trick if you get the following answers:

Do you want to be thinking about this?
    YES   (NO)

Would you prefer to be thinking about or doing other things?
    (YES)   NO

Does thinking this lead to feeling bad in the pit of your stomach?
    (YES)   NO

Would you want a good friend to have this thought?
    YES   (NO)

4. Empower your daughter to fight back against OCD lies instead of being ruled by them. Explain that trying to ignore OCD thoughts usually takes more work for the brain and ultimately results in the OCD thoughts having more power. It is helpful to see OCD for what it is—a liar—and refuse to play its games, rather than tiptoeing around OCD as if it had something important to say.

I frequently have scary thoughts that I have to try to get out of my head. Sometimes this works, but other times it doesn't. My family thinks I should get professional help—should I?

Having intrusive, unwelcome, bizarre, or scary thoughts causes emotional distress and makes it harder to focus on living your life. Like many people, your gut reaction to these negative thoughts is to try not to think them. This process is known as **thought suppression**. Unfortunately, a good deal of research shows that thought suppression is not an effective strategy. As in your situation, it might work sometimes, but it doesn't work all the time. You can't just turn thinking off in any reliable manner. At best, thought suppression is a short-term gain/long-term pain strategy. Even if trying not to think something scary works for a little while, the frightening thought usually returns. A common example of the paradox in thought suppression involves asking people not to think about a pink elephant. For someone given these instructions, a pink elephant is usually the first thing that comes to mind. Similarly, when you try to make yourself not think about your daughter being kidnapped, for example, you might end up having this thought even more.

For more long-term, effective results, seeking cognitive-behavioral therapy is a good idea. Learning to carefully identify, evaluate, and more helpfully respond to your negative thoughts can be very beneficial. Perhaps you are routinely overestimating danger and underestimating your ability to cope—through therapy and practice outside of therapy sessions, you can learn to think more realistically. In addition to questioning and disputing negative thoughts, a very strong strategy (especially for OCD) is facing the thoughts you fear—this is known as exposure. When you force yourself to repeatedly confront the thoughts and images you have been avoiding, you allow yourself the chance to become desensitized or habituated to these thoughts. In other words, your anxiety will usually decrease after an adequate period of contact with the feared thought.

To accomplish desensitization in treatment, you might listen to an audiotape of your scary thought repeated over and over. Alternately, you might make a tape of your frightening image carried out to the worst-case scenario, and then listen to this tape at least once a day. The idea of purposely recording and listening to your scary thoughts or images might sound strange, but it is one of the best ways of helping you to face them so that they bother you less.

I worry that saying certain words aloud will hurt my family. My therapist says that these are OCD thoughts and not *my* thoughts. How do I convince myself of that?

Notice that when you are experiencing obsessions, there is another part of you that knows the thoughts are not accurate. We call the obsessions **OCD lies** (the thinking produced by your illness) and distinguish these from *your own thoughts*. For the sake of getting better, you need to practice separating your own thoughts from OCD lies, and then turning the volume up on your thoughts and the volume down on the OCD thoughts. OCD thinking is frighteningly creative and tricks people into believing all sorts of bizarre things, such as:

- I have to turn the light switch on and off 12 times to make sure my husband gets home from work safely.
- If I think Tim might have a car accident, then he'll have one.
- Unless I say this exact prayer 5 times before I go to sleep and right when I wake up, my son will fail his midterm.
- I have to wiggle the door handle 33 times before I can be sure that it is locked.

Knowing that OCD lies to you is a very important tool in fighting the disorder. Similar to the ideas listed above, your belief that saying certain words out loud will result in harm to a family member has a "magical" quality to it. For combating OCD, however, a diligent effort to consider evidence and reason is essential. For example:

- How exactly does your saying certain words bring about harm to anyone?
- Logically, how would that work? What are the mechanisms?
- Are you God?
- Just because you think something (and everybody thinks strange things at times!), does that make it true?

Disputing and challenging OCD tricks is vital! Even more important than questioning OCD thoughts, however, is exposing yourself to your obsessive fears. Gradually making yourself say the words that you are scared to say is essential to getting better. You will feel very anxious at first, but this anxiety will subside over time. The more you allow yourself to keep saying the words, the more you will become desensitized, or habituated, to the fear of vocalizing the words. The more you say the words, the more you will get to see that your prediction that a family member will get hurt is incorrect. In contrast, if you keep insisting that you not mention certain words because of your fear, these words and OCD maintain a hold over you. Avoidance is any anxiety disorder's best friend!

I don't understand how making myself think my scary thoughts will help me. Can you explain this?

To really understand how exposure works, let's look at an example of jumping into a very cold swimming pool. The cold water can feel shocking at first. So, suppose you hate the cold feeling and you immediately get out of the pool—how will you feel? You'll probably feel better—relieved. Now, what if you have to get back in the pool? How will that feel? Most likely, you will feel stunned again by the striking cold. If you keep getting in and out of the pool, you will feel temporary relief each time you get out, but each time you jump in, it will be pretty jolting. This in-and-out pattern is similar to what happens when you have a scary thought, suppress it, then have it again: you feel a jolt of fear each time.

Now, suppose you jump in the very cold pool for the first time without letting yourself immediately climb out. What do you think will happen? What will occur is a process called habituation, or desensitization. You won't like the cold at first but you will get used to it and less bothered by it by staying in the pool rather than escaping from it. The same is true with unpleasant thoughts.

Chapter 13

UNDERSTANDING POSTTRAUMATIC STRESS DISORDER

- What is posttraumatic stress disorder?
- How common is PTSD?
- How does PTSD develop?
- Does everybody who goes through a traumatic event develop PTSD?
- What can people do to help cope with traumatic experiences?
- What can make the effects of a trauma worse?
- I have been told that I have PTSD. Does that mean that I am crazy?
- What are some common thoughts that people suffering from PTSD have?
- How do I know if I need professional help for my symptoms from trauma?
- I have made arrangements to work with a cognitive-behavioral therapist on my PTSD. What can I expect?
- I have heard that a therapy called EMDR can help people who have been through a trauma. What is EMDR, and can it help me?
- I think I have PTSD. Are there any medicines to help me with this?
- How do I know if my child has PTSD?

What is posttraumatic stress disorder?

According to the diagnostic manual, DSM-IV, **posttraumatic stress disorder,** or **PTSD,** involves the following:

1. Exposure to a traumatic event in which the person: a) thinks she or someone else is going to experience serious injury or death, and b) feels intense fear, helplessness, or horror.
2. Repeated re-experiencing of the trauma, in the form of intrusive thoughts, nightmares, flashbacks, or extreme distress when exposed to reminders of the traumatic event.
3. Persistent avoidance of any stimuli associated with the trauma. There is also a general numbing of emotional responses. People may report they can't feel loving feelings, or just don't enjoy the things they used to.
4. Persistent symptoms of hyperarousal. This might be shown through decreased sleep, increased irritability, outbursts of anger, difficulty concentrating, an increased startle reflex, and panic attacks.
5. For a PTSD diagnosis, the duration of the re-experiencing, numbing, and hyperarousal is at least one month. The same symptoms occurring for less than a month would be diagnosed **acute stress disorder.**
6. These symptoms must cause the individual clinically significantly distress or impairment in their social, occupational, or academic functioning.

Examples of traumatic experiences that may result in PTSD include rape, assault, car accidents, wars, fire, mining accidents, or natural disasters, such as floods and earthquakes. There is some evidence to suggest that traumas caused by people, such as violent crime or rape, are more difficult to cope with than natural disasters.

How common is PTSD?

PTSD rates seem to vary depending on the type and duration of the exposure to a traumatic event. Whereas about 75% of the population in the United States is exposed to one or more life-threatening traumatic events at some point, only about 25% of these individuals progresses to full-blown PTSD symptoms. Here are some data from different studies.

- For rape victims, the range for the development of PTSD was 35% to 80%.
- The lifetime PTSD prevalence rates for Vietnam Veterans and prisoners of war held by the Japanese in World War II are 31% and 50%, respectively.
- About 12% of accident victims develop PTSD.
- About 32% of cancer patients and 30% of HIV patients exhibit signs of PTSD.
- Overall, community prevalence rates for PTSD symptoms probably range between 6% and 9%.
- Twice as many women (10.4%) as men (5%) develop PTSD at some point in their lives.
- Men most often develop PTSD in response to rape, combat exposure, or childhood physical abuse or neglect.
- For women, sources of PTSD most often include rape, physical attack or being threatened with a weapon, and childhood sexual or physical abuse.

How does PTSD develop?

Here is a model based on the work of Foa and her colleagues: When a trauma occurs, a **fear structure** is formed in memory. This fear structure includes three parts:

1. **Stimuli** of the trauma (sights, sounds, odors, sensations of the event)
2. **Responses** to the trauma (physiological and emotional responses to the event)
3. **Meanings** attributed to the stimuli and responses.

When people face reminders of the trauma, they experience unpleasant memories and symptoms that feel distressing. To relieve this distress, PTSD sufferers try to avoid trauma-related cues. However, while trying to avoid or escape from stimuli that produce intense negative emotions, these people struggle with the *meaning* aspect of their fear structure. They have great difficulty incorporating their new beliefs about events with their previously held strong life assumptions, and the inability to reconcile the conflicting views (a process known as **accommodation**) promotes the maintenance of PTSD symptoms:

Sample of pre-trauma beliefs	Sample of post-trauma beliefs
The world is safe and predictable.	The world is scary and unpredictable.
My life is controllable.	My life is out of control.
I can cope with the things that happen to me.	Danger can occur at any time, and I can't cope.

In general, PTSD sufferers feel driven to make sense of what happened because it goes against their pre-trauma beliefs. However, if they try to make sense of the meaning of the trauma, this also activates the emotional response part of the fear structure, which can feel terrifying and overwhelming. So, the pull is between trying to make sense of the trauma and attempting not to think about it. Foa and her colleagues believe that hyperarousal (anxiety) results from the tension between struggling to find meaning from the event while trying to avoid reminders (including thinking) about the event.

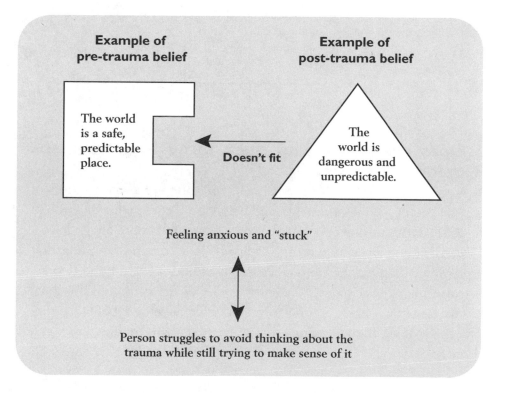

Like a puzzle, people with PTSD have great difficulty reconciling their new beliefs with their old assumptions—they can't "make the pieces fit," which often results in considerable distress if left untreated. Cognitive-behavioral therapy can be very useful in helping people develop more integrated, balanced thinking that promotes moving forward rather than staying stuck.

More realistic post-trauma belief

The world is a safe place, but there are no guarantees, and bad things sometimes happen.

Does everybody who goes through a traumatic event develop PTSD?

Very harmful or life-threatening situations often produce a variety of unpleasant feelings, thoughts, and behaviors. People who go through traumas often re-experience the scary event, feel more angry, have a harder time sleeping, and try to avoid being around anything that reminds them of the trauma. People may also feel guilt and depression following a trauma. Despite a variety of common emotional reactions to a severe trauma, not all people develop PTSD.

First of all, the following types of trauma are more likely to result in PTSD:

- A more severe, prolonged, and unexpected life threat
- A threat caused by human behaviors rather than natural disasters
- Experiences that force the person to behave contrary to his values

Second, the following personal factors are associated with an increased vulnerability to PTSD:

- Female gender
- A genetic predisposition toward emotional disturbance
- History of psychiatric illness, such as depression, anxiety or personality disorders
- Childhood trauma
- Lower intellectual ability
- Recent life stressors or changes
- Feeling a lack of control over one's life
- Recent excessive alcohol or drug intake

Finally, an important buffer against the development of PTSD is social support. When people have someone with whom they can discuss the trauma, they do better than when they keep their feelings and thoughts to themselves.

What can people do to help cope with traumatic experiences?

Following the events of September 11, 2001, the Academy of Cognitive Therapy provided a list of dos and don'ts that may help with the impact of a trauma. Here are the dos:

Stick to your normal routine so that you can increase your sense of predictability and control, which will make you feel more secure and safe.

Talk with your family and friends for support. Research consistently shows that having a support system in place serves as a good buffer against the harmful effects of the traumatic experience.

Manage day-to-day conflict responsibly to prevent strain and irritability from causing more problems.

Find ways to relax. This might include exercise, yoga, prayer, or meditation. Find the approach that works best for you.

Talk about the events and experiences with people close to you. Collective grieving may be helpful if a trauma has been widespread.

Find time to be involved with leisure and recreational activities. People often feel guilty about enjoying themselves after a trauma. However, returning to a routine and finding enjoyment are very important for coping with the aftermath of a trauma.

Try to be compassionate with yourself. Remind yourself that the occurrence of the traumatic event doesn't undermine your sense of worth, competence, or lovability.

Allow yourself to go into situations that remind you of the trauma. Face the people and the places you associate with the traumatic event even if your anxiety is high when you do so. The more you face your fears, the more you develop the power to diminish them.

Remind yourself that you cannot control everything and that there is no certainty in this world; however, you can still live a very full, meaningful life.

Try to view the future with some optimism. You recover more quickly when you think about a traumatic situation as time-limited and not necessarily an indication of what is going to happen in the future.

Remind yourself of how resilient human beings are. According to research, most people who experience trauma recover within a few months. Let yourself believe that you will feel better.

Recognize when you need professional help and be willing to seek it. After a trauma, suffering on your own may exacerbate the negative effects of the trauma. There are valuable treatments to help people overcome anxiety and depression following a trauma.

What can make the effects of a trauma worse?

The Academy of Cognitive Therapy suggests the following don'ts:

Do not repeatedly watch upsetting television news reports if you believe it is increasing your anxiety.

Try not to run away from or suppress your painful thoughts. The more you try to suppress these thoughts, the more you actually think them.

Try to think realistically about the possibility of danger vs. the feeling that danger is inevitable now that this traumatic event has occurred.

Try not to make the problem worse than it already is by constantly assuming that the worst will happen.

Do not avoid the situations that remind you of the trauma. The more you avoid, the more the anxiety is perpetuated in the long-run.

Do not turn to unhealthy escape behaviors to cope, such as using alcohol or excessive sleeping. Escape behaviors may actually increase your anxiety over the long-run.

Try not to judge yourself for the way you are feeling after a trauma. Remind yourself that anxiety, depression, and anger are common after a trauma, and they often decrease on their own. Beating yourself up for having these emotions just worsens the whole situation.

Do not blame yourself for something you believe you should have done or not done. You could not see into the future. You did not know what was going to happen. Blaming yourself exacerbates your distress.

I have been told that I have PTSD. Does that mean that I am crazy?

People with PTSD suffer from a good deal of anxiety and tension, and they can feel as if they're going crazy. They may get depressed as well. Sadly, some get into drugs or alcohol to treat themselves. However, crazy or psychotic usually refers to losing your grip on reality; life becomes governed by fiction—an imagined reality that only you know about. People suffering from psychosis can have hallucinations; PTSD sufferers may have flashbacks. The difference is that these flashbacks are actually vivid images of the traumatic event that force themselves into the sufferer's mind. Still, though the images are painful to think about, the PTSD victim knows what is real and present and what is a painful memory. So, no, PTSD does not mean you are crazy. It is helpful to remember that symptoms of PTSD are prolonged versions of a *normal* reaction to an *abnormal* situation.

Keep in mind that often, the feeling of going crazy stems from feeling out of control. Traumatic memories intrude even if you try to guard against them. Ironically, the memories can intrude all the more *when* you try to guard against them. This is why the best way of regaining control is to face the trauma through therapy.

What are some common thoughts that people suffering from PTSD have?

As a result of a very frightening or life-threatening traumatic event, people can begin to think in distorted and harmful ways. Some of the common thoughts that go along with PTSD include the following:

- "It's my fault that the trauma happened. I should have known it was going to happen. I should have done something to stop it."
- "If I were a stronger person I could handle this better."
- "I can't get over this pain. I can't cope. Something bad will happen at any moment."
- "I can't trust anyone."
- "I am weak and helpless."
- "The world is dangerous. Nothing will ever be good again."
- "If I lost control, it would be horrible/life-threatening/intolerable."
- "After all I've been through, I deserve special treatment."
- "Others are out to get me. Others won't protect me."
- "If I don't follow the rules, I could die." (This is commonly experienced by combat veterans, who may obsess about following the rules, a concern left over from the life-or-death implications of combat.)

PTSD sufferers may often be unaware of these thoughts, so treatment involves both identifying the thoughts and replacing them with thoughts to help move beyond the trauma.

How do I know if I need professional help for my symptoms from trauma?

If you feel like your social, occupational, or academic functioning is suffering as a result of your experience from the trauma, then it is a good idea to seek professional help. You don't have to meet every symptom listed to justify talking with a mental health professional. Often, just telling the story of the traumatic events is very beneficial, especially when you are able to speak to a neutral party outside of your family or friends. If you are experiencing the following, treatment can help:

- You are constantly "on edge" or irritable.
- You have difficulty responding emotionally to the ones you love.
- You can't sleep.
- You have started to use alcohol or other drugs to cope.
- You are making yourself unusually busy to avoid the effects of the trauma.
- You have upsetting memories or nightmares.

Strongly consider consulting a clinician if you don't have anyone to talk to, don't feel safe talking to your family or friends, or are overly focused on protecting loved ones form hearing your experience.

I have made arrangements to work with a cognitive-behavioral therapist on my PTSD. What can I expect?

Early in treatment, you can expect to discuss PTSD, treatment rationale and specific goals. Treatment may include the following:

- **Interoceptive exposure** may be a first step to help you desensitize to the physical symptoms of panic. If you recall from chapter 7, this technique involves creating your own panic attacks to take the power out of them.
- **Imaginal exposure** involves vividly recreating the details of the trauma with the guidance of a therapist. This technique is important for helping you become desensitized to the feared memories. A hierarchical (or step-by-step) approach is used to help you gradually confront the avoided memories. Imaginal exposure first occurs in the therapist's office, and is followed up with homework, such as writing down and regularly reading your trauma story. Alternately, an audiotape of the traumatic event can be made for listening to at home. This idea might sound very strange or terrifying to someone who has suffered a trauma. However, the more avoidance—the more problems persist; facing fears leads to desensitization to the fear. (Think of watching a horror movie on the 100th vs. the first time or jumping into a cold swimming pool and getting less bothered by the cold vs. repeatedly getting in and out and feeling just as cold or colder each time.) We want "hot" bad memories to turn into just bad memories.
- **In vivo exposure** then helps you become desensitized to actual aspects of the traumatic situation—for example, the place where the trauma occurred—through a gradual and collaborative approach.

- **Cognitive restructuring** helps you think more realistically and helpfully about the trauma, your role in it, and future implications. Here are some examples of ways you may change your thinking:

Negative Self-Talk	More Realistic Self-Talk
It was all my fault I was raped.	It was the rapist's fault, NOT MINE.
I should have offered to drive her.	I couldn't have known that drunk driver would be on the road. We would probably both be dead, and the kids need me.
I could have done something to prevent that machine from falling on him.	None of us knew that machine would malfunction. It weighed a thousand pounds. I couldn't have stopped it from falling.
Something bad is bound to happen.	I can't see into the future.
I'll never feel okay again.	It may take time and work, but I can start to feel okay again.

- **Anxiety management techniques** (progressive muscle relaxation, breathing retraining, visualization, and distraction) are also used to improve your coping.

I have heard that a therapy called EMDR can help people who have been through a trauma. What is EMDR, and can it help me?

EMDR stands for eye movement desensitization and reprocessing. The idea behind EMDR is to recreate the kind of eye movements you experience while dreaming in order to reduce the intensity of distressing memories and feelings. The standard treatment involves the following phases:

Phase I: History-taking and assessment of readiness for EMDR. Client and therapist identify possible targets for sessions, such as a smell or visual image that recalls the distress of the trauma.

Phase II: Evaluation and enhancement of client's coping skills in preparation for EMDR.

Phase III: During the treatment, the therapist has you move your eyes back and forth, by following the movement of her hand, while bringing a specific traumatic memory to mind. In addition to repetition, there is also a cognitive component. Here you identify a negative belief about yourself associated with the trauma, and eventually substitute a preferred positive belief. After several trials, the memory no longer generates such horrible feelings.

Phase IV: Closure. The therapist asks the client to keep a journal to note any relevant material that comes up during the week, while employing self-soothing activities learned in Phase II.

Phase V: Evaluation of sessions and progress.

Many people say that their anxiety, terror, or humiliation fades after EMDR sessions. Today, therapists sometimes employ repetitive tapping in place of eye movement, or use headphones that alternatively repeat a pleasant sound in each ear.

Because EMDR focuses directly on traumatic memories, adverse reactions can occur and generally have to do with memories coming to mind following sessions. It's a good idea to confirm that your therapist has completed advanced EMDR training and has experience in selecting clients and successfully conducting EMDR. Careful evaluation of your ability to tolerate the treatment is especially important if the trauma was severe or prolonged. Depending on your history, the type and severity of the trauma, and your psychological make-up, treatment length ranges from three to twelve or more EMDR sessions.

Research has supported the benefits of EMDR, though it is unclear as to why it actually works, and it remains a controversial treatment. Some studies suggest that positive effects may be due to the exposure and desensitization to traumatic memories.

I think I have PTSD. Are there any medicines to help me with this?

The good new is that several medications can help. Antidepressants particularly the SSRIs, are probably the best at relieving symptoms of PTSD. Medicines in this group include Prozac, Luvox, Paxil, Zoloft, Celexa, Lexapro, and Effexor (similar to an SSRI). The downsides are that it can be challenging to determine the most effective one for you, and it can take several weeks to see the benefits. Medicines that can work faster are the benzodiazepines like Valium, Xanax, and Klonopin. Unfortunately, these medications can easily lead to dependency. Researchers are also exploring the use of Clonidine, a high blood pressure medication, and beta-blockers such as Inderal.

Although medications can relieve symptoms, they cannot be counted on fully to restore you to your usual self. It takes a lot of work on your part as well. It's best to get professional help from a psychiatrist, psychologist, or counselor. A psychiatrist can prescribe medication, though some provide therapy and some do not. If not, you can obtain a referral. Many clients work with a therapist while periodically consulting with a psychiatrist regarding their medications. The psychotherapy is usually essential for a full recovery, as is doing a lot of "homework." Ultimately, people do best when they systematically expose themselves to the traumatic situation—when they face their fears. The use of psychotherapy, medication, and often a support group makes it easier to do this.

Even when you are successful with treatment, it is possible that at some future time, probably when life is particularly stressful, the symptoms may return. Don't despair, though, because you can re-learn therapeutic strategies fairly quickly. It usually takes a shorter period of time to get back on track.

How do I know if my child has PTSD?

Any event that is perceived as life-threatening and results in great fear, helplessness, or horror can be the cause for PTSD. Children usually express their horror and fear with disorganized and agitated behavior at the time of the incident. Later, the memory of the event might be repeated in themes of play activity and in nightmares, though children may not be able to report what went on in the dream. Upon exposure to elements of the trauma, a child may react with great anxiety and engage in avoidance behaviors. If told he must go to the place where the trauma occurred, he may suddenly get dizzy or complain of a stomachache. The same may apply if he is asked to discuss the event. He may develop difficulty remembering the incident or parts of it. He may also avoid contact with friends or playful and fun activities with family members. Some children believe in a foreshortened future —"I won't become an adult." Others develop omen formation—the belief in an ability to foresee future unpleasant events.

If you see these kinds of changes in your child, seeking professional help from experts in child psychology or psychiatry is important. Talk therapy doesn't always work for kids, so therapists often let children express themselves with games, toys, and play. Though not often used, medications given to adults with PTSD may be necessary to relieve symptoms in a child. Involving your child in activities that empower him and strengthen his self-concept (e.g., a scouting group or martial arts class) may also be valuable.

Chapter 14

COMMON PTSD REACTIONS

- Since I was assaulted, I am scared all the time. I'm embarrassed that I can't get past this. What is wrong with me?

- Why do people distance themselves from loved ones after a trauma?

- I have PTSD, and my biggest problem seems to be my guilt for surviving while others came out worse. Is this a common feeling?

- I hate that I am a victim of a trauma. I can't think of what happened without getting furious. Does this sound like PTSD?

- I was in a car accident; now, I'm afraid to drive. What should I do?

- My husband will soon return from active war duty. I know he's been through a lot. What can I expect when he comes home?

- How can I support a family member returning from active combat?

- I got so little sleep while stationed overseas, I thought I'd sleep for days after returning. Instead, I can't settle down to sleep. Why is that?

- My brother came back from active combat feeling emotionally crippled. He's been drinking a lot and looks so sad to me—almost lifeless, without any joy or enthusiasm. Should I get involved?

- What causes flashbacks, and how can I make them stop?

Since I was assaulted, I am scared all the time. I'm embarrassed that I can't get past this. What is wrong with me?

What is wrong is that you were assaulted, and your system is still responding to the trauma you experienced. Stress and anxiety following a trauma are *normal* responses to an *abnormal* situation. When you went out that day, you didn't expect to be assaulted. The experience of the trauma probably included feelings of helplessness, and perhaps you thought you were going to die. This kind of event is hard for the mind to process, and intense emotion goes along with it. You might be torn between trying not to think about the assault and trying to make sense of what happened or why it happened.

Your embarrassment about your symptoms is not uncommon; however, avoiding the problem will only add to it. Research has revealed that the best way to get past the effects of trauma is to face the trauma in a safe setting with a therapist or support group. Sometimes it is hard to admit that a trauma still affects us; yet, doing so is a first step in getting better.

Why do people distance themselves from loved ones after a trauma?

The kinds of traumas that lead to PTSD are not only upsetting in their own right, but also tend to upset the worldview of the victim. The faith most of us have in life being basically good and rewarding is shaken at its core for the trauma survivor. As a result, the survivor is afraid to emotionally invest in what used to be most important to him—even his own partner, children, or favorite sport. Almost unconsciously, he shuts his emotions down as a way of protecting himself from getting his faith and hope stolen away again. The thinking may be, "If nothing means anything to me, then I don't have to worry about losing it." Fortunately, most people improve from PTSD on their own within about 6 months. A sizeable minority, however, suffer from it long-term. Treatment, of course, improves the odds.

Obviously, the disorder not only causes suffering to the victim but also to those who love him and feel like he's turning into a person who is either cold or mean. It's common for loved ones to feel hurt and discouraged, if not downright angry. They may also be on pins and needles worrying when the next shoe will drop. When others start to become anxious and share the victim's suffering, we call this **vicarious traumatization**. For all these reasons, it is important for loved ones to seek support themselves as well as to assist the victim in getting help.

I have PTSD, and my biggest problem seems to be my guilt for surviving while others came out worse. Is this a common feeling?

Yes, and all too often. Survival guilt is a common reaction to events where one feels spared and others died or were hurt badly. It seems to be part of many people's makeup to feel so badly for others and to worry that others may resent them for being spared. PTSD usually involves a lot of anxiety and tension or the opposite—emotional numbness. But guilt like you describe is common too. The guilt can be a serious barrier to treatment as one may feel he deserves to suffer. Another emotion common to PTSD is shame. PTSD leaves us feeling so strangely out of control that we may feel ashamed and humiliated by our perceived inability to control our minds.

We can also feel foolish for getting ourselves into situations that led to a trauma. For example, you may blame yourself for a wreck, even if you weren't driving. You may say to yourself, "If only I hadn't gone to the party that night, I never would have been in that wreck. How foolish I am for having gone. How guilty I am for having been spared." On examination, this kind of thinking is illogical, but for some of us it is hard to shake. The shame can interfere with therapy as well. Sometimes people can't easily go out into public, feeling sure that others are judging or mocking them.

Hopefully you can take assurance in the reality that you are not alone with these feelings and pursue relief from your lingering distress. A PTSD support group—available in your community or through the Internet—can link you up with others who are struggling with similar concerns, and therapy can help you replace guilt-inducing beliefs with more accurate and loving statements about yourself. Some examples of these statements might be:

- If I were hurt, that would not make things better, but would only add to the grief of loved ones.
- I could not have predicted that this would happen.
- It is good that I was spared.

I hate that I am a victim of a trauma. I can't think of what happened without getting furious. Does this sound like PTSD?

Anger is a common way to protect ourselves from danger. It is also a frequent aspect of PTSD. We all have a tendency to protest when things don't go our way. Some individuals downright rage against what happened to them, though—and to what is *still* happening to them. PTSD victims remember grueling details of their trauma, to dream about the same, to react with terror if they see something in the corner of their eye resembling the traumatic situation, and to ask the unanswerable question, "Why me?" So, of course, anger becomes part of the picture.

If you are truly concerned you could harm someone as a result of your anger, you need to protect both yourself and others by getting assistance. A psychiatrist can help you evaluate this concern and prescribe medications, or even hospitalization, if needed. Of course, if a crisis feels imminent, it is always appropriate to call 911. More often, the anger is hurting you, disguising other painful feelings.

When people experience something as profound as you have, we can feel angry because it seems that no one else "gets it." Not feeling understood can generate resentment. Or, sometimes we may be so ashamed of our vulnerability that we stay angry as a way of scaring people away. Though the anger is understandable, it is ultimately a poor solution because it alienates us from the help we need. Letting people into our lives is better for healing. Find a PTSD support group. They can be located in your area or even on the Internet. The chances are that someone there will "get it."

It is important to note that a **support group** is a self-help method, whereas a **therapy group** for PTSD would have a trained facilitator with expertise in PTSD and group dynamics. Some people feel safer in a therapy group, knowing that there is a trained leader to help guide the process. Others may prefer a support group alone or in combination with individual therapy, while some prefer to just work with a therapist. The important thing is to find the help that feels both safe and responsive to your needs.

I was in a car accident; now, I'm afraid to drive. What should I do?

Keep in mind that after a trauma like a car accident, it is common for people to avoid situations or stimuli that remind them of the trauma. So, after a motor vehicle accident people often are reluctant or afraid to drive. They may have predictions like "If I get in the car again I'll have another wreck" or "Since I had that accident I know I couldn't cope with another one." Obviously, these predictions generate a good deal of anxiety. In order to avoid the anxiety generated by these predictions, it makes sense that people would resist driving. However, the more you avoid driving, the more your negative predictions become entrenched and keep you from driving.

Learn to question some of your negative predictions. There are no guarantees in life, but you want to look at the data about your driving record. How many times have you driven? How many accidents have you had? You may be talking about one accident in a record where you have driven 20,000 times or more. Being willing to study the facts can help you look at the situation in a more balanced manner. Whereas generating more realistic thinking about driving is important, a crucial aspect of this problem is getting back into the car and driving. It is beneficial to do this in a graded or gradual way. In other words, you start with small steps that get you closer to the car and get you driving. Gradually, you work your way up to more challenging tasks. You can break this down into as many steps as you like, but the key to getting over your fear of driving is to eventually get yourself in the car and drive.

My husband will soon return from active war duty. I know he's been through a lot. What can I expect when he comes home?

As much as they want to be home, war veterans can initially encounter difficulties in making the adjustment to the calmer, more predictable reality of life outside of the battle zone. If he was exposed to combat, the chances of difficulty are greater. Here are some of the challenges that can arise:

- In order to distance himself from the trauma of war, the veteran may become emotionally numb, and family members can feel cut off.
- His feelings may surface as irritability.
- He may have a diminished interest in sex and distance himself from you.
- You may notice a watchfulness on his part, and a focus on protecting your family from danger.
- He may have difficulty sleeping or relaxing.

It helps to be prepared for these possibilities so that you don't take them personally. The transition can be hard for family members who are so eager to connect with the returning veteran. Often, these stress symptoms diminish in the days and weeks following the veteran's return. If, however, he experiences significant distress or difficulty functioning—or if symptoms continue or worsen—he is likely to be suffering from a more serious reaction.

How can I support a family member returning from active combat?

First of all, you help by being there. The presence of family members can help diminish social withdrawal on the part of the veteran. Family rituals, such as having dinner together, attending worship services, and engaging in holiday traditions help to anchor the veteran with a sense of normality and predictability.

Don't take things personally. When the veteran distances herself or becomes irritable, keep in mind that these are normal reactions to the lingering stress of combat.

Take care of yourself. In order to remain supportive, you may need a place to work out your frustrations. Remember the basics of nutrition, exercise, and rest.

Be informed. Further information and support are available through your nearest Veteran's Administration, and the National Center for PTSD has an extremely informative website at www.ncptsd.org.

Offer to help. Let your returning family member know that you are willing to listen (and be prepared—listening to stories of trauma can be stressful for the listener as well). Male veterans, in particular, may not find it natural to discuss feelings in a focused way, but they may come up in another activity. Taking regular walks or golfing together—without an expectation that you talk—can provide the kind of comfort that makes the words come more easily. While talking about the trauma and associated feelings is very helpful, forcing it tends to backfire.

Provide information. Sometimes veterans feel they are going crazy if they experience flashbacks or nightmares. Reassure your family member that this is a *normal* reaction to an *abnormal* situation, not a sign of weakness or instability. On the other hand, you also help by telling your loved one when you think he needs professional assistance.

Participate in the veteran's treatment. If your loved one is in significant distress or having difficulty functioning, encourage her to seek help *and* go with her. Acute stress disorder and PTSD are very treatable, and early intervention can prevent needless distress.

Accept help from others. Allow yourself to embrace the support of military and civilian friends, especially those who have been through situations similar to yours. Make use of the community resources available through your church, military base and government organizations for veterans and their families.

I got so little sleep while stationed overseas, I thought I'd sleep for days after returning. Instead, I can't settle down to sleep. Why is that?

Sleep difficulties are common following active military duty. Here are some of the reasons:

- Even though you have returned, your brain may still be operating as if you are on the lookout for danger. Biological changes associated with the fight-or-flight response may still be operating, keeping your heart racing, senses activated, and not allowing you to settle down and relax.
- Worry about sleep can contribute to the problem. Thinking "This is terrible. I *have to* sleep!" only escalates your level of anxiety and makes it harder to sleep.
- The use of alcohol or drugs can interfere with sleeping.
- Nightmares can bring back past traumas and put them into the present, upsetting you and making it difficult to return to sleep. Likewise, the avoidance of feelings and memories can keep you from settling down.
- Injury or health concerns can interfere with sleep.

- Sensitivity to the slightest sound or motion, a skill you developed in duty, may persist and make you a light sleeper.

For general tips on promoting sleep, see chapter 16. If trauma-related symptoms linger, consult with a professional for evaluation and treatment.

My brother came back from active combat feeling emotionally crippled. He's been drinking a lot and looks so sad to me—almost lifeless, without any joy or enthusiasm. Should I get involved?

Two complications of PTSD are depression and substance abuse or dependence. Sometimes the symptoms of PTSD are so impairing that the sufferer starts to feel helpless, hopeless, and depressed. Depression is an equally impairing psychiatric illness, and, especially when combined with substance abuse, can lead to suicide. Alcohol impairs judgment and gives people a false sense of courage, while making them less inhibited. Whatever restraints a person may have sober are gone with intoxication.

Your brother needs treatment if he is not already getting it. His therapist should be told of his depression and drinking, and asked to conduct a suicide assessment. He may need hospitalization or chemical dependency treatment to help him stabilize, and possibly, to save his life. Sometimes the most merciful thing a family member can do is to commit a loved one for treatment, even if it's against the sufferer's will. We have many successful treatments today, including medicines and psychotherapy. With help, your brother has a good chance of getting better.

What causes flashbacks, and how can I make them stop?

Flashbacks seem to emerge from the way the brain stores traumatic memories. Normally, we "play over" troublesome events in our minds until they cause us no trouble. We become desensitized to the event because of the repeated thoughts or because we have found some solution to the crisis. This thought repetition is in the form of memories, or verbal stories, not as images. Traumatic flashbacks are different. They play like a videotape of the event. They repeat, too, but instead of losing their power to scare or distress us like normal troublesome memories, they overwhelm us over and over again. It's like we can't get used to the event.

Sometimes psychiatric medicines help in stopping flashbacks. Antidepressants called the SSRIs can be useful, but they are better in relieving the emotional numbing and excessive arousal symptoms of PTSD. Lithium or an anticonvulsant called Tegretol may be beneficial. A beta-blocker called Propranolol has also helped veterans decrease intrusive images from combat exposure.

Ultimately, we need to process our experiences, and flashbacks can make this a challenging prospect. Working with a professional with whom you feel safe is key. A PTSD therapy or support group can also be a helpful way to share information with others who experience flashbacks.

Here are some techniques people use to interrupt flashbacks:

- Humming a song, reciting a favorite poem, or reciting a list of favorite facts aloud
- Focusing on a wall and moving your eyes from one bright object to another, shifting the speed of movement to avoid a routine
- Holding an ice cube in one hand and clasping it strongly, offering a competing sensation to the memory

- Splashing ice-cold water on your face (This automatically produces the "diving reflex." The heart rate lowers, blood pressure rises, and circulation is shunted to the body's core. The brain is shocked and immediately distracted.)
- Having a friend count randomly aloud, sometimes using words where numbers would be expected (i.e., "One, two, three, ten, five, six, seven, flower, nine, dog" and so on).

Chapter 15

ANXIETY AND LIFE CHALLENGES

- How can anxiety affect the relationship with my partner?
- How can anxiety affect my relationship with my kids?
- How does anxiety affect my work?
- How do life transitions contribute to anxiety?
- I hear the term "midlife crisis" used a lot. What is a midlife crisis?
- What are some good ways of coping with midlife changes?
- I am over 70 and find myself worrying more than I used to. What is this about?
- My husband makes me anxious when he waits to pay our bills. He doesn't miss any due dates, but I think he should pay them sooner. What can I do?
- My dad has been diagnosed with Alzheimer's dementia. I'm so worried about him that I can't seem to enjoy anything anymore. What can I do to make this better?
- What can I do to help with my anxiety about taking tests?
- I am waiting to hear if I got the job I interviewed for. Waiting is driving me crazy! How can I manage my anxiety in the meantime?
- What behaviors might be helpful as I wait to hear about the job?
- What can I do to help with anxiety about dating?
- I have a hard time turning anyone down. This problem is making me very anxious. What can I do about it?
- Can I qualify for disability if I have an anxiety disorder?

How can anxiety affect the relationship with my partner?

Anxiety may affect close relationships in a variety of ways. Here are some common scenarios:

1. An anxious person may feel more anxious if his partner is not around. He may become clingy and demand the partner remains close by. Some anxious individuals believe they must have a "safe person" near at all times. The partner may want to distance from the clingy behavior, which makes the anxious person more anxious, then more clingy, and a vicious cycle begins.

2. If the anxious person is worried about the other's safety, he may not only demand the loved one stay close by, but also check in frequently. He may insist that his partner do things in a very specific way that leaves the anxious person believing the other will be safe. Sometimes the anxious person becomes irritable if others don't follow his instructions. The partner may experience the anxious person as domineering, intrusive, and unreasonable.

3. An anxious person may frequently look to his spouse for reassurance about his fears and worries. To accommodate the anxious spouse, the partner might provide reassurance that gives the anxious person relief. However, this relief is only temporary and sets up a pattern of reassurance-seeking in the relationship. This can become very annoying to the non-anxious partner.

4. Some individuals are attracted to anxious people because of a need to be needed. The anxious spouse may be seen as a wounded bird. In these cases, trouble may occur if the anxious spouse receives successful treatment and no longer needs the other as much.

5. Some anxiety problems leave a person feeling detached from others, and the partner may feel neglected. If the anxiety is

more than distressing and becomes disabling, the partner may be required to take on more of the family responsibility. The partner's response to this situation may range from becoming angry over the unfairness of this extra obligation, to feeling guilty about not doing enough, to finding solace through escapist behaviors like drinking or leaving the relationship altogether.

How can anxiety affect my relationship with my kids?

Just being in a home where there is a prevailing sense of tension and worry tends to rub off on kids. This is where addressing your own anxiety is a gift to your children as well as yourself. Here are some ways anxiety can affect the parent-child relationship:

1. Anxious parents may become overprotective as they worry to excess about their children's safety. Some children may enjoy the extra attention, although they too may overidentify with the anxious parent and become anxious themselves. Others may rebel and keep their distance from the anxiously protective parent.

2. If the parent is overwhelmed with anxiety and has functional impairments, a child may prematurely assume the role of a caretaker. Concern for the parent can hide an inner resentment about having to take on this role. Feelings of anger can then bring on feelings of guilt—a mix that generates a great deal of inner turmoil.

3. Sometimes, it's the child who brings anxiety into the family system. This may be the case with a particularly sensitive child who has less tolerance for stress and disorder. Parents can respond by being overprotective of the child or, at the other extreme, can distance themselves out of frustration.

4. In some cases, the parent-child relationship can become defined by shared avoidance. Activities are kept within the home and family, and social outlets are limited or nonexistent. This arrangement can be a foundation for a phobic response to the relationships and challenges of the outside world.

When the relationship with your child or children feels stressed or unhealthy, family therapy can be a valuable resource. Individual therapy can also provide parents a place to face their anxiety and work through it so it is less likely to rub off on the children.

How does anxiety affect my work?

The best part of anxiety is that it can motivate us to do our work. Too much anxiety, however, can interfere with our performance. Here are some ways that can happen:

- We may become preoccupied with worry at the expense of work tasks.
- The consequences of anxiety, such as fatigue, low energy, and muscle tension, make it difficult to do our work.
- We can't complete our work due to distraction, hesitation, doubt, and indecision.
- We become so concerned about performance that we fear exposing our work products to others. This leads to procrastination and sometimes immobility.
- Social phobia may lead to avoidance of important interactions with coworkers, and ultimately to avoidance of work.

When we can't fulfill our responsibilities due to anxiety, this can have a powerful impact on our self-concept, leading to feelings of worthlessness and possibly clinical depression. This may be especially true for men, who tend to have stronger identifications with their work life and, even in our liberated society, still feel internalized pressures to be the good provider for their families.

How do life transitions contribute to anxiety?

Many theories have described specific life stages and the adjustments that need to occur between them. Research across different cultures and eras, however, has challenged the general applicability of these socially prescribed life transition periods. For example, many of today's couples may still be raising kids when the theory prescribes an "empty nest" crisis.

Yet, it makes intuitive sense that the challenges of growing can generate anxiety. For example, going from infancy to toddlerhood includes the frustration of trying to coordinate the body to walk when the mind is ready to run. Transitioning from early to later childhood means leaving home for large stretches of the day for school. Adolescence then poses the new challenges of romance and lust. The stress of life decisions in early adulthood gives way to the responsibilities of work and raising a family.

What happens when you have invested so much in raising a family, and now the children are nicely on their way to taking care of themselves? Whereas some of us may have a party and celebrate having more time for travel and personal interests, others may experience difficulties in adjusting to less parental involvement. After being so oriented toward the children, the question of "What now?" may generate stress and discomfort, at least temporarily. These same questions can also arise when a person has mastered and become bored with his life's work.

Although transitions present their own challenges, they also present opportunities for growth and desired change. The trick is to accept the initial awkwardness that comes with transition, to draw on past successes for strength, and to open yourself to change.

I hear the term "midlife crisis" used a lot. What is a midlife crisis?

"Midlife crisis" is a popular term that studies have shown to be more of a myth than a reality. The good news is that research on the emotional stability of men and women in middle age suggests that on average, they do not necessarily experience surges in distress during the typical "empty nest" or "midlife crisis" periods. In fact, well-being appears to generally stabilize over the lifespan.

Even so, the accumulated wisdom regarding midlife can be helpful to those who enter a period of questioning and confusion about their lives. In this sense, "midlife" is not so much defined by an age, but by a person's own journey. It is a point where you have accomplished the big things you set out to do in early life, such as settling into a career, raising a family, or just "specializing" in a certain way of living. Now you're at a time where you're looking at it all and deciding if this is what you really want. You may be struck by the realization that you have limited time left and want to make it count.

A Swiss psychiatrist named Carl Jung believed that midlife is the time when we can bring to life the "opposites" within us. An extroverted person may turn inward and take up gardening or painting. A shy person may crave more interaction and even begin to show off a bit. Surprisingly, the qualities we are discovering are often ones we've devalued. As a shy person, I may have told myself I didn't want to be like those loudmouths who mingle at parties. Now I'm changing my tune. Who am I anyway? Concerns about identity can leave us feeling unanchored and anxious. Other factors, such as physical aging, hormonal changes, retirement questions, and shifting family roles, can add to this identity challenge. Some of us at this time may feel we are drifting and in need of a change, something to get some zip back. While this could lead to the stereotyped response of acquiring a sports car and a young lover (more myth than reality-based!), it is as likely to lead to a personal renaissance.

What are some good ways of coping with midlife changes?

First, being willing to acknowledge changing thoughts, feelings, and goals is important. Second, you might look at the shifting winds of midlife as a call to make improvements in your life that you have been postponing. Midlife is a common period to enter therapy, as people tend to be in a more reflective place at this time of life. It also helps to share your experiences with others who may be going through similar circumstances. As you exchange stories with family and friends, you will feel less alarmed by what you are experiencing, and may even be able to see the humor in it. Sometimes it helps to talk to an older friend who has gone through similar changes. Finally, the following stress relievers are tried and true:

Insight. Understanding why you're feeling unsettled and learning from that can turn your "crisis" into an important opportunity.

Socialization. Sharing can transform difficulties into connections, and bad days into entertaining stories.

Realistic Thinking. You can benefit from learning to look at your situation, your strengths and weaknesses, and your goals in more balanced, accurate ways.

Exercise. A proven antidepressant, exercise helps boost your mood, energy level, and sexual desire.

Rest. Sleep deprivation can trigger the same symptoms as depression and anxiety. A lack of adequate sleep makes problems seem larger, interferes with clear thinking, and increases irritability. A balance of active days and restful nights promotes good mental and physical health.

Make sure to talk with your physician about illnesses and their complications, as well as medications and their side effects. Resist the temptation to "blow off" these concerns, as a simple change in treatment can often make a world of difference. Last, it's not uncommon for people who have been alcohol drinkers for a good part of their adult lives to start becoming more dependent on alcohol later in life. Doing an inventory of what you put into your body is always a good idea.

I am over 70 and find myself worrying more than I used to. What is this about?

Often, older individuals struggle with more medical problems, more responsibility for taking care of not only themselves but ill spouses, less than adequate incomes, and unsafe housing. Their spouse may have died, and they must do the things their spouse always did, including the cooking, cleaning, shopping, bill-paying, house maintenance, or yard and car maintenance. They may feel ill at ease with these new roles and responsibilities.

As we age, we often feel more vulnerable if our bodies don't work as well. We may not see, hear, or move as well. We may feel considerably weaker and less able to defend ourselves adequately. We may find it embarrassing to think of others witnessing us in these compromised states. Also, people who used to give us a feeling of security may have died, or become ill or enfeebled. Our protectors may not be there. Our minds may not be as sharp, and our memories may not serve us as well. All these factors may conspire to undermine our sense of managing things in a way about which we can feel good.

Whereas increased stressors can largely contribute to increased worrying, it may be a good idea to determine if you have an underlying medical disorder or if you are taking any medicines that may cause anxiety symptoms. Also keep in mind that the American Psychological Association is working on ideas that make it more likely that older adults are willing to pursue and follow through with effective psychotherapeutic treatment.

My husband makes me anxious when he waits to pay our bills. He doesn't miss any due dates, but I think he should pay them sooner. What can I do?

Keep in mind that nobody makes you anxious. You make yourself anxious based on what you are telling yourself. Think about what you say to yourself when your husband doesn't pay the bills exactly when you want him to. Do you say "This is terrible!"? This is the kind of self-talk that feeds anxiety. To help you feel better, you can learn to look at the situation in a less upsetting way. If he is not missing any due dates, then what is the problem with his waiting to pay the bills? If you really want your husband to be responsible for the bills, you can free yourself by allowing him to use his own system. Maybe you haven't completely given over responsibility to him; in your mind, you may blame yourself if the bill is sent later than you wish. Try letting go of the whole thing, and say to yourself, "It's not my problem—he's taking care of it." Then focus on the tasks that are your responsibility. Or, if you really want to be in charge of the bills, offer to take on the task. Problems in relationships often arise when we try to control another person's behavior. What you can control is your own behavior (e.g., by paying the bills yourself) or your response to your partner's behavior (e.g., by changing your self-talk).

The bottom line is nobody makes you anxious. You make yourself anxious—and you can free yourself from anxiety, too.

My dad has been diagnosed with Alzheimer's dementia. I'm so worried about him that I can't seem to enjoy anything anymore. What can I do to make this better?

In a difficult situation like your dad is facing, you're obviously going to be concerned and sad. You love him and don't want him to suffer. However, we often turn concern into ruminative, unproductive worry that interferes with work, relationships, and emotional and physical health. Although you can't undo your dad's condition, you can learn to think about it in a less anxiety-provoking way. Your improving your self-talk about this situation is very important in coping with it better. Think about what you're telling yourself now. Is it something like the following?

Distressing, unhelpful thoughts:
- I have to make this better for him, and I can't.
- This is the worst thing that has ever happened—we can't get through this.
- I should have done something to prevent this from happening to him.
- To be a good daughter, I have to worry about him.
- Since Dad can't enjoy things as much anymore, I shouldn't enjoy things either.

If this is the type of internal dialogue you're having, then it's not surprising that you would feel anxious, depressed, and guilty, and be unable to enjoy things. You've set up some impossible demands for yourself. Would you talk to your best friend this way and impose these same rules on her? Or, would you recognize that her self-care is important, too, and want her to take better care of herself? You might be better off applying the comforting words you would say to a friend to yourself. There's no doubt your dad's illness is upsetting, but certain ways of thinking can help you manage it better or worse.

Less distressing, more helpful thoughts:
- I'll do my best to help him, but there are limits to what I can do.
- This is very sad, but we will get through it.
- There was no way I could have prevented this from happening, but I can do things now to help Dad.
- Excessive worrying about Dad doesn't make me a better daughter—it just makes me feel overwhelmed.
- I can be concerned without this ruining my life.
- I'll be in a better position to help Dad out if I'm taking care of myself, too.

Learning to think more realistically and less rigidly about this situation is important to keep your emotions from becoming extreme. Self-care behaviors are also essential. Some people feel too guilty to arrange pleasurable activities when a family member is ill because they think this is selfish. Remember there is a huge difference between *selfish* (where you disregard or violate others' needs and wants to further your own agenda) and *self-care* (where you recognize that in order to carry out life's tasks effectively, you need to be attending to your own care adequately).

What can I do to help with my anxiety about taking tests?

Test anxiety is a common problem with which people struggle. If you have the goal of making a good grade in a class, scoring a certain level on a college admission test, or passing a certification exam, you naturally want to do well on the test. Being concerned enough to prepare adequately for the evaluation is certainly in your best interest. However, keep in mind that tests in and of themselves do not make a person anxious. Rather, your self-talk about exams and your behaviors determine how nervous or how calm you feel before and during a test.

Adequate preparation is also a key to managing test anxiety. The following is a list of behaviors that tend to help before the test.

- Attending classes
- Finding out what's expected on the test
- Taking good notes and reviewing them regularly
- Reading the material carefully
- Scheduling uninterrupted time to study
- Studying in a place without distractions
- Pacing your studying (rather than cramming)
- Making flashcards or outlines to emphasize the main points
- Asking for help when you don't understand the material (perhaps getting a tutor)
- Getting involved in a study group
- Rewarding yourself *after* studying instead of before or during, which can prolong procrastination
- Practicing relaxation techniques
- Getting adequate sleep, nutrition, and exercise

Anxiety-Generating Self-Talk	Anxiety-Reducing Self-Talk
I must make a perfect score.	I'll do the best I can—demanding perfection from myself just makes me more nervous.
I'll never learn all this material—I'm going to fail.	I'll break the chapters down into manageable parts and learn as much as I can. Telling myself that I'll fail is unhelpful.
When I bomb this test, my teacher will see how stupid I am.	I have no way of knowing that I'm going to bomb this test, and my teacher is not going to judge me completely on the basis of one test.
Doing poorly on this test will show everyone that I'm a failure.	One test cannot make me a failure, regardless of my score.
Everyone else has prepared much better for this test than me.	Focusing on what others have or have not done doesn't help me—I will focus on doing my best on this test.
I can't take tests—I always get too nervous and my mind goes blank.	Although it's been difficult in the past, there's no reason I can't take tests. Even when nervous, I can still function and answer test questions. I'll do better if I'm patient and willing to write down the parts I do know. The more I write, the more I'll remember what I want to say.

During the test, you want to maximize your opportunity to give your best performance. It's a good idea to scan the test, carefully read the directions, and get an idea of how to pace yourself. Complete the easiest questions at the beginning. Mark questions for which you don't know the answer—you will want to come back to these rather than wasting a lot of time worrying about them. If you start to feel anxious and draw a blank, remind yourself that you have studied and the answers will come to you. It's a good idea to write down anything you remember related to the question—this can trigger the answer in your mind. During the test, also remember to use relaxation strategies to calm yourself as needed.

I am waiting to hear if I got the job I interviewed for. Waiting is driving me crazy! How can I manage my anxiety in the meantime?

If the job is one you strongly desire, it's very common to feel impatient about the outcome. Obviously, you want to know if you got the job or not, and the sooner the better. However, this is a good time to consider what factors you can and cannot control. The job interview is done, so you can't change that. Ruminating about your performance in the interview—whether you said or did something you wished you hadn't—will probably just make you more anxious or even discouraged. However, you might jot down things you learned from this interview that you want to be sure to remember for next time. Keep in mind that you don't determine what the employers are looking for. Many things besides just the resume or interview influence hiring decisions. Remind yourself that you can't control what choice the employers are going to make.

What can you control? Your current thinking and behaviors! What you tell yourself post-interview will determine how anxious you feel:

Anxiety-Generating Thoughts	Anxiety-Reducing Thoughts
Waiting is driving me crazy!	Waiting is uncomfortable, but I can tolerate it.
I can't stand not knowing.	I don't like not knowing, but I can stand it.
What if they didn't like my answers?	I don't control their reactions to what I said. I did my best at the time.
I probably didn't get the job.	I don't know whether or not I got the job.
What if nobody wants to hire me?	People have hired me in the past. I will find work again.
I *must* get this job.	I *want* this job, but there's no reason I must have it.
If I don't get it, it will be terrible!	It will be disappointing, but not the end of the world.

It is easy to become immobilized during a waiting period. Yet, this can be a time to open other doors so you don't put all your eggs in one basket. It can also be a good time to look at your own feelings about the potential job. It's so easy to focus on how we are being evaluated that sometimes we forget to consider our own feelings about the situation. It is always helpful to clarify what we want and don't want.

What behaviors might be helpful as I wait to hear about the job?

After an interview, some type of follow-up is often appreciated. You can do this in the form of a thank-you letter to let the potential employers know how much you appreciated their time. You can also reiterate why you think you are well-suited to the job. (Do this tactfully and with moderation—obviously, you don't want to nag the interviewers!)

Additionally, you might consider having a fifteen-minute worry time each day. Here, you set aside a specific time to think of nothing else but the job—the interview, comments you made, the idea of not getting the position. By giving yourself permission to focus on this worry for a prescribed amount of time, you are freeing up the rest of the day. When worries related to the job pop into your mind, you forcefully tell yourself—"I'll deal with that in my worry time, not now!"

Finally, remember that we live in a society where everybody wants quick results. None of us likes to wait, but waiting is a part of life. Distracting yourself with pleasurable activities (e.g., taking a walk, going to a movie or the gym, meeting a friend for coffee, attending a church event) can be very beneficial. It's also a good idea to continue your job search—remember this is not the only job that you could enjoy doing.

What can I do to help with anxiety about dating?

Dating anxiety can arise from any of the factors listed or a combination of them:

1. Exaggerated fear of rejection/criticism
2. Perceived deficits in social skills and negative self-focused attention
3. Actual deficits in social skills
4. Previous experience with unpleasant dating situations
5. Avoidance of dating opportunities

Basically, individuals with dating anxiety may not have the communication skills important for negotiating a dating relationship or they may *think* that they don't have the necessary communication skills and act accordingly. Or, negative dating encounters in the past may have been paired with anxious feelings to the point that someone doesn't want to even try dating again, perhaps out of dread of rejection. The more this person avoids dating, the more the self-defeating beliefs become entrenched, and the anxiety is perpetuated.

A famous tale in psychology is Albert Ellis's (founder of Rational Emotive Behavioral Therapy) self-practice in which he forced himself to ask out 100 women in Central Park in New York City. He only secured a few dates and some of those women didn't show up, but he succeeded in desensitizing himself to the effects of rejection! In fact, the assignment of asking for dates from individuals you are sure would say no is often a psychotherapy assignment. (If the person agrees to the date, that's great, too!) The experience of purposefully getting rejected teaches people "Even if I don't like it, I can stand to ask someone out and get turned down." Despite the initial discomfort, learning to tolerate rejection is liberating and essential for less upsetting dating. To reduce dating anxiety, how you think about dating is just as important as your actual dating experiences!

Anxiety-Generating Self-Talk	Anxiety-Reducing Self-Talk
Nobody would ever want to go out with me.	I can't know if someone would like to go out with me until I ask.
I just can't talk to members of the opposite sex—I never know what to say.	It's initially uncomfortable for me to talk to members of the opposite sex, but I can learn skills to help me. The more I practice, the easier it will get.
It's awful to be rejected.	It's inconvenient to be turned down, but not the end of the world. This is a part of dating!
I can't stand to have a bad date—why even bother?	Having a bad date is disappointing, but I can stand it. I can consider this date to be practice in dating and in figuring out what I want and don't want in a partner.
Dating shouldn't be this hard. There's something wrong with me.	I wish dating were easier, but dating involves some level of difficulty for everyone!

While learning to think less catastrophically about dating is vital, having a repertoire of adequate dating skills is also extremely important. Perhaps it is true that you really don't know what to say to members of the opposite sex and this causes you to feel very self-conscious. The good news is that dating communication strategies can be acquired! Social skills training can include initiating small talk, learning how to effectively exchange compliments with a member of the opposite sex, non-verbal means of communication, assertiveness training, talking about feelings, managing periods of silence, practicing how to ask for a date, and negotiating physical intimacy with a partner. Using videotapes in social skills training can help you see how you come across, allowing you to increase the behaviors you like while reducing those you don't. Using calming breathing and relaxation strategies can also be very beneficial in improving comfort with dating. For people getting back to dating after divorce or loss of a partner, Laurie Helgoe's book, the *Boomer's Guide to Dating (Again)* provides step-by-step guidance.

I have a hard time turning anyone down. This problem is making me very anxious. What can I do about it?

Problems with saying no or setting limits with others can certainly lead to difficulties with anxiety. Learning to say no may not be a behavior with which you are comfortable, but that doesn't mean you can't do it. When we refuse to turn down a request, it is often because we are having certain thoughts about the idea of saying no. These thoughts may include:

- "It would be horrible to tell that person no."
- "I can't hurt anybody else's feelings."
- "If somebody asks me to do something, I should always help out."
- "A real friend would say yes."

If you operate with these kinds of rules, it makes sense that you would go ahead and do something you are asked to do, even if you don't want to do it. Learning to respond honestly means first learning to challenge your rules about what it means to say no. Instead of thinking it is awful to say no, remind yourself that even real friends have to decline favors sometimes. You can also say to yourself, "If I become resentful of the people I am helping, this will hurt my friendships even more than occasionally saying no." This kind of self-talk is more likely to motivate you to say no and maintain good feelings about your relationships. You also may want to look at what you've learned about saying no from parents and other adults. It's easy to automatically take on the behaviors and beliefs of those we've observed, rather than to decide for ourselves what makes sense.

Refusing to say no can result in a very full, perhaps overextended schedule. If you map out your obligations and notice that you have very little recreational or leisure time for yourself, it is not that surprising that you struggle with being anxious. The assertiveness questions and time monitoring activity in later chapters can help you take steps to get more of what you are wanting, and less of what you are *not* wanting, from your life.

Can I qualify for disability if I have an anxiety disorder?

Any illness that is disabling may make you eligible for disability from insurance companies or the government. Because mental illnesses are diagnosed through self-report and observations of patient's behavior rather than through laboratory testing, disability agencies are more demanding of proof for psychiatric illness. Most anxiety disorders are quite distressing and clearly interfere with daily functioning. It is rare, however, that they create disability on their own. More often, the disability occurs when several mental disorders are present, and together result in severe impairment.

Although obtaining disability may resolve some problems, there are psychological risks to taking this step. Anxiety disorders generate feelings of self-doubt and incompetence; being labeled "disabled" can add to this stigma. Being on disability also tends to promote more avoidance behavior, and avoidance is one of the strongest contributors to continued anxiety. Often, financial problems might be somewhat improved with obtaining disability, but one's emotional well-being might be more compromised. Make sure you have exhausted other resources before considering this step.

Chapter 16

CALMING YOUR ANXIETY

- I've been told I'd feel better if I could learn to accept my anxiety. How am I supposed to accept something that feels so horrible?
- Can practicing meditation help me with my anxiety?
- Can exercise help with anxiety?
- Can owning a pet help my anxiety?
- Does what I eat affect my anxiety level?
- Can writing in a journal help with my anxiety?
- What are some practical tips to help me start journaling?
- Can massage therapy help with my anxiety?
- I do fine all week, even though I work long hours and have a lot of responsibility. Then, on Sunday, when I'm supposed to rest and relax, I become anxious. Isn't this a little backwards?
- Why do I get so anxious when I have to make decisions? It doesn't seem to matter whether it's a big or small issue—I hate having to decide!
- How can I remind myself of more helpful ways of thinking?
- I've heard that most people are sleep-deprived. Is this true, and does sleep loss lead to anxiety?
- What are some ways I can improve my sleep without medications?
- What type of self-talk can I use when I work myself up trying to fall asleep?
- I become extremely anxious when I have to confront someone or say "no." I end up doing things I don't want to do just to avoid disappointing others. Why am I such a wimp?
- My friends tell me it's no big deal if I say no or ask for what I want, but it is a big deal for me. Why is it so hard?
- How do I keep from feeling uncomfortable when I want to tell someone "no" or ask for what I want?
- What are some daily activities I can schedule to reduce my anxiety?

I've been told I'd feel better if I could learn to accept my anxiety. How am I supposed to accept something that feels so horrible?

When you are willing to accept a situation, you stop working against reality. If you feel anxious, telling yourself "I can't stand this" and "This shouldn't be happening to me" only adds to your anxiety. Accepting your anxiety is not the same as *liking* your anxiety—it only means you are willing to tolerate it. Consider Beck, Emery, and Greenberg's acronym A.W.A.R.E to help you remember key strategies for coping:

A: Accept the anxiety. Try saying, "Okay anxiety, come on; this is a hassle, but I can manage." With this attitude, you'll find that your body actually feels better over time and you actually upset yourself less. Try not to hate your anxiety or beat yourself up for being anxious. A common saying in the treatment of anxiety disorders is "If you are *not* willing to have it, then you will."

W: Watch your anxiety. Just observe the anxiety without judging it as terrible. Notice when your anxiety goes up and down like waves in the ocean. Anxiety is time-limited—it cannot stay permanently. By watching the anxiety, you realize that it does go down. The more you can detach yourself from the anxious symptoms, the less bothered you will be.

A: Act with the anxiety. This may sound pretty tricky. When people are feeling anxious they sometimes think that they can't function, they can't do their job, they can't drive, they can't take care of their children. These ideas are untrue. It is uncomfortable to experience the anxious symptoms, but you can safely go about your normal activities. It is important that you let yourself see this. Go ahead and do what you need to do, even with the anxious symptoms. You can slow down if you need to, but don't avoid doing the normal tasks. The more you avoid, the more the anxiety gets a hold over you.

R: Repeat the steps. Beck and colleagues encourage people to continue to accept their anxiety, watch it, and act with it until it decreases to a more tolerable level.

E: Expect the best. You've probably noticed that what you fear the most very rarely happens. In the morning, when you are lying in the bed worrying, tell yourself, "I don't know what is going to happen, but I'll handle it." Don't expect to function throughout the day with no anxiety, but let yourself know you can get through the day successfully even with anxious symptoms.

Can practicing meditation help me with my anxiety?

Many activities, such as muscle relaxation and exercise, help reduce or better manage anxiety. Meditation works a different way. It teaches us to embrace any emotion we experience, whether painful or joyful. The idea is that if one allows a full experience of any emotion, she can let go of it easier and faster and find a new one it its place. People feel emotionally richer and less stuck if they meditate regularly. In addition, clinical trials with meditation have revealed reductions in blood pressure, cortisol (the "stress hormone"), cholesterol, and cardiac arrhythmias.

Jon Kabat-Zinn's work at the Center for Mindfulness at the University of Massachusetts Medical Center has helped people with severe chronic pain and emotional problems, including anxiety disorders. Through regular mindfulness meditation practice (e.g., sitting and noticing your breathing, scanning your body to observe what you're feeling, some types of yoga), people become more accepting and less judgmental of their life experiences, including times of suffering. Individuals come to see that life is a series of moments—rehashing the past or worrying about the future interferes with appreciating the fullness of each moment that they have. At the heart of this program is increasing awareness and the understanding of the value of being versus doing. In meditation practice, the following attitudes are emphasized and encouraged (source: *Full Catastrophe Living* by Jon Kabat-Zinn):

Non-judging: Observe your experience without the habit of judging it as good or bad.

Patience: Appreciate that each experience is your life at that moment without rushing to change things or thinking that you need to make events better.

Beginner's Mind: Be willing to look at things through new eyes without assuming you know everything. Realize that each moment is unique.

Trust: Trust in yourself and your own wisdom without constantly trying to conform to others and their standards.

Non-striving: Allow yourself to "be" without trying to reach any particular goal.

Acceptance: Allow yourself to see things as they are instead of being blinded by how you think things should be.

Letting Go: Practice letting go versus holding on to experiences so that you can more fully be in the present.

These values are also helpful in responding to your anxiety symptoms. Through a regular practice of meditation, people learn to observe their thoughts, feelings, and behaviors without becoming caught up in them. Mindfulness encourages seeing anxious thoughts as mental events (not necessarily reality) and developing a more accepting, less demanding relationship with the thoughts and the feelings.

Can exercise help with anxiety?

We've all heard that exercise helps a person feel better. This idea might sound good, but many people have great difficulty when it comes to implementing an exercise program. Clearly appreciating the benefits of exercise might increase your chances of trying it. Numerous research studies have revealed how valuable exercise can be for improving anxiety, depression, stress management, sleep, physical self-concept, and physical health—the benefits of exercise have been *proven* repeatedly. Mechanisms through which exercise is helpful include the following: increased blood flow to the brain, biochemical changes such as the release of endorphins that elevate mood, distraction from worries, and development of a sense of mastery in a physical activity.

When beginning an exercise program after obtaining approval from your physician, keep in mind that your anxiety level might increase during the first few minutes of the workout. However, as you continue to exercise, the anxiety will subside. By the conclusion of the exercise, your anxiety level will be lower than before you started. Several studies have referred to exercise as having a "tranquilizer" effect on anxiety.

To get started with an exercise routine, here are some tips:

- Choose an activity you will enjoy. Some options include walking, jogging, aerobics classes, strength training, dance, yoga, tennis, golf, basketball, and volleyball.

- Consider doing your exercise choice with a friend or a group to increase your enjoyment of the activity and your motivation to do it regularly. Alternately, many people prefer to pair their favorite music with their workout.
- Begin the activity slowly and proceed carefully. Try not to get impatient and do too much at once. Remind yourself that it is preferable to increase your exercise intensity and duration at a gradual pace rather than an abrupt one. Pay attention to your body's reactions.
- Try to do some form of exercise at least 4–5 times per week. Realize that as you continue to exercise regularly, the activity will become more of a habit about which you can feel good than a chore.
- Give yourself credit for your exercise efforts. Individuals often benefit from keeping an exercise log to chart their improvements. It can be particularly helpful to monitor anxiety levels before and after a workout so that you can see how exercise helps your mood.

Can owning a pet help my anxiety?

There is some research to suggest that interactions with animals can reduce symptoms related to stress and anxiety. For example, studies have demonstrated that just petting an animal reduces blood pressure, and one study showed that this benefit continues even when the pet is not present. Another study found that watching fish swimming in an aquarium worked just as well as hypnosis in reducing anxiety in patients awaiting surgery. Pets may be helpful after surgery as well—pet owners exhibit faster recuperation time when recovering from operations, and actually have a higher survival rate after serious illness. An Australian study found that cat and dog owners needed less medication for cholesterol, blood pressure, sleeping difficulties, or heart problems.

Some of the activities involved in caring for a pet, such as walking your dog, may also reduce stress. Pets keep us company and provide a sense of well-being. The responsibility for a pet may distract us from our own concerns and worries. Certainly, many people regard pets as being like family. We all desire to feel needed and cared for. If you live alone, the addition of a pet may help to meet these needs, increasing your sense of comfort and reducing anxiety.

Does what I eat affect my anxiety level?

Consuming a lot of caffeine can make you more anxious. Nicotine may do the same, though many people say they feel calmed by nicotine. The relaxation we feel after a Thanksgiving dinner is due to the amino acid tryptophan, which is found in turkey and milk. This substance is a precursor of serotonin, and has been found to induce calm and promote sleep. The wisdom of having a glass of milk at bedtime seems to have some basis. There also appears to be value in having smaller and more frequent meals as a way of maintaining blood sugar levels, thus keeping moods and energy more even.

We all have psychological associations with certain foods, and many of us can list our favorite "comfort foods." These foods may or may not be good for us, but they provide a sense of psychological comfort. For example, if your mother lovingly served you chicken soup when you were feeling bad, you may feel calmed and comforted when you have chicken soup as an adult.

Can writing in a journal help with my anxiety?

When we go through hard times, we often just want to forget these painful experiences. Society provides us many distractions—alcohol, movies, books, theme parks, and television. We have studies, however, that demonstrate symptom improvement in people who write down their difficult experiences and the feelings that come with them. It may be that, by just putting the feelings on paper, we are able to back away from the intensity of the situation and better evaluate things. Often, we are able to sort out feelings and reach insight and clarity through writing. Also, writing slows us down, which is a real benefit to anxiety sufferers. Lab tests reveal reductions in heart rate and blood pressure, as well as drier skin, in people who have just finished writing. All of these changes are associated with relaxation.

"Therapeutic journaling," or writing down your feelings and concerns, has been associated with reductions in symptoms of depression and anxiety. In fact, research by James Pennebaker found that immune function was enhanced for study subjects who wrote about their deepest feelings as compared to subjects instructed to write about trivial matters.

Journaling can also be a useful tool for therapy, increasing your awareness and providing helpful material for the sessions.

What are some practical tips to help me start journaling?

Keep in mind that therapeutic journaling is for your use, so you don't need to be concerned about how your writing comes across to anyone else. Here are some recommendations for how you can get the most out of journaling:

1. Create a time and space for journaling. Set aside 15 to 20 minutes each day when you will not be disturbed, choose a place you feel safe and comfortable, and have a notebook or journal and pen ready in that place.

2. When you sit down to write, start with what you are aware of at the moment. You can either take the approach of just writing what comes into your mind (free association) or more actively exploring the feelings you are aware of. You can grapple with a problem or concern, getting to specifics, such as "when do I feel this way?" or "what is it about that situation that still bothers me?"

3. Give yourself lots of permission to let go of punctuation, grammar and organization. If you try to make your journal into an elegant essay, you interfere with the flow of your writing. For now, think of your journaling as a discovery process. If you like, you can go back and work it up into a story format later.

4. Strong emotions may emerge as you write. It is usually helpful to stay with these feelings and write through them, as getting at the more difficult emotions tends to provide the most benefits. Do allow yourself the option of consulting with a therapist if the feelings become overwhelming. It is also helpful to link the feelings to specific events and thoughts. Keep in mind that repeated exposure to upsetting memories, even in imagination, helps diminish the impact of those memories.

5. If you have a hard time journaling without structure, there are many structured journaling books available to help guide you (see the Resources section later in the book).

6. Therapeutic journaling is meant to free you up to live your life, not to be a substitute for life. Journaling becomes counterproductive if it is used as a way to escape or avoid the relationships and responsibilities in your life.

7. Remember, your journal is yours alone. Only you can decide whether you want to share any of your entries and, if so, how you share them.

Can massage therapy help with my anxiety?

Different people have different preferences for how they get relief from anxiety. Whereas developing more realistic self-talk is very important for reducing anxiety, incorporating helpful behaviors is just as necessary. Massage therapy has been used to help people suffering from problems with arthritis, pregnancy, depression, and breast cancer, to name a few. Investigating the results of over 30 scientific studies, researchers found that one session of massage therapy helped decrease state (temporary) anxiety, blood pressure, and heart rate. Further, repeated sessions of massage therapy produced reductions in trait (long-term) anxiety, depression, and long-term pain. Benefits may also stem from the client expecting treatment to go well and from having a good rapport with the massage therapist. If massage therapy is something you want to consider, it's a good idea to make sure that your therapist is licensed. You may want to ask for recommendations from your family physician or friends who have had massage therapy.

I do fine all week, even though I work long hours and have a lot of responsibility. Then, on Sunday, when I'm supposed to rest and relax, I become anxious. Isn't this a little backwards?

You aren't alone. People with anxiety problems often feel better when they are engaged in productive activities—this can serve as a good distraction from worrying and focusing on bodily fluctuations. However, this is only a temporary solution. Inevitably, there will be some down time, and you want to be able to enjoy it rather than dread it. Here are some factors that contribute to "Sunday anxiety":

1. If you have a rigid rule that "I'm supposed to rest and relax—I shouldn't feel this anxious," you can set yourself up for feeling anxious. Remember, the more one tries to resist anxiety, the more the anxiety usually persists. It would probably be better if you could get in the habit of telling yourself, "So what if I'm a little anxious? I can still find ways to enjoy the day." You also might want to question the rule that you "have to" relax—maybe a vigorous game of tennis better fits your mood.

2. Alternately, you may be thinking, "I have things to do—I really shouldn't be just resting." Again, this type of self-talk will put pressure on you, leading to more anxious feelings. Practice giving yourself permission to be completely unproductive.

3. Another thing that can happen is that you may notice more physical fluctuations in your body when you are at rest. You might notice your heart beating faster than what you think is normal, then become alarmed, then notice your shallow breathing, become more alarmed, and so on. Your heart is likely to be beating at the same rate as other times; you are just more tuned in.

4. Finally, if you are in fast-mode all week, it takes a little time to settle down. It is not uncommon to feel anxious or even a little depressed or bored when you slow your pace. This can happen on vacations as well, where it takes a little time to get used to a slower, more relaxing tempo. Let the negative feelings just roll over you like a wave, and give yourself time to adjust to the down time. It may also help to build more down time into your week, and start relaxing on Saturday rather than waiting until Sunday. Practicing the transitions in your pace will help you downshift more easily.

Why do I get so anxious when I have to make decisions? It doesn't seem to matter whether it's a big or small issue—I hate having to decide!

Decisions in and of themselves don't make a person anxious. Your self-talk about decision-making determines your emotional reaction and influences your behavior. Often, when people feel anxious about making a decision, they are saying to themselves something along the following lines:

- I don't know what to say—I should know, and it's terrible that I don't.
- I have to make the right decision.
- If I make the wrong choice, it would be terrible.
- I always have to make sure my decisions please my family, friends, etc.

If the above examples resemble how you're thinking about a decision, then it's not surprising that you would feel anxious and avoid or delay making decisions. You're putting tremendous demands on yourself to meet your own or someone else's very high standards.

To feel less anxious about decision-making, you would benefit from talking to yourself differently about your choices. Some more helpful, realistic self-talk might include:

- Given what I know at this point, I'll make the best decision I can and I'll deal with it.
- There's almost never just one right decision, and certainly no perfect one.
- If this choice turns out to be problematic, it would be uncomfortable, but I could cope.
- I can't make sure my decisions always please anyone else—that's up to the other person. If he or she doesn't like my decision, it might be inconvenient, but it's not the end of the world.

If you learn to inflict less unhelpful pressure on yourself about making decisions, there's a good chance that you would feel concern instead of anxiety. Further, if your emotion were concern, you'd probably have more resources for making a better decision compared to when you are anxious.

Whereas changing self-talk is a big part of reducing your anxiety about decisions, you might also benefit from improving your problem-solving skills in this area. Running a cost-benefit analysis is a great tool to aid in decision-making. Rather than just tossing around "what ifs?" in your mind, which can feel exhausting, consider putting your ideas on paper. All choices have advantages and disadvantages—it can be very productive to have these written out so that you can weigh them and make your choice with more confidence. (See Appendix A for worksheet.)

How can I remind myself of more helpful ways of thinking?

Coping cards are used to help people remind themselves of more helpful, realistic thinking at times of increased susceptibility to excessive anxiety, depression, anger, and other extreme negative emotions. The idea here is to use a 3" x 5" (or larger) notecard to serve as a prompt to "stop and think" versus just being mislead by unhelpful emotional reasoning. On one side of the card, write down the negative automatic thoughts that lead to unwanted feelings and behaviors. On the other side of the card, write more realistic, helpful, and balanced statements that are more likely to lead to manageable emotions and useful behaviors. Many people keep their cards with them in their purse, datebook, briefcase, wallet, or pocket. Others prefer to post their card somewhere prominent, like in their car, by their computer at work, on the refrigerator, or by the bathroom mirror. The most important aspect of using coping cards is that you look at your card actively and frequently. Remember changing thoughts requires diligent practice, but the emotional and behavioral improvements make this work worth it! Here's what your cards will look like:

I've heard that most people are sleep-deprived. Is this true, and does sleep loss lead to anxiety?

Sleep disturbance is the third most common patient complaint in doctors' offices, behind headaches and colds. Over 40 million Americans suffer from long-term sleep disorders each year, and 20 million Americans experience occasional sleeping problems. Sleep disorders cost $16 billion in medical expenses each year and more in indirect costs such as lost productivity. If people want to use medication to improve their sleeping, benzodiazepines are often prescribed, with the recommendation for short-term use only. Some

One side of card:

My negative thoughts/predictions:

Resulting Feelings/Behaviors:

Other side of card:

My more realistic, balanced, coping thoughts:

Resulting Feelings/Behaviors:

antidepressants can also have a sedating effect that improves sleep. However, medication should not be the only intervention for sleeping problems. There are many things people can do to help themselves, without medication. Keep in mind that sleep is a habit, and it takes time to change it. Fortunately, the research on sleep disorders has provided a wealth of information on how to correct sleep problems. In the case of anxiety, one of the most important habits to change is the way we talk to ourselves while settling in to sleep. Getting worked up and concerned about sleep loss backfires, so learning to talk to ourselves in soothing and reassuring ways is key.

What are some ways I can improve my sleep without medications?

- Maintain a regular sleeping and wake-up time. Even if you get less sleep than you would like, get out of bed at the same time each day and don't allow yourself to sleep in on weekends.
- Don't watch the clock. Once you've set the clock for your waking time, turn it away from you or place it somewhere out of sight.
- Decrease or eliminate daytime naps.
- Exercise daily but not within 4 hours of bedtime.
- Get sufficient exposure to bright light during the day.
- Use the bed only for sleeping or sex. Don't use your bed for paying bills, eating, reading or watching television.
- Do not use bedtime as worry time. Tell yourself "I can deal with that concern tomorrow." Keep a small notepad by your bed where you can jot down a couple of words that will remind you the next day of any important ideas.
- Try a relaxation technique or a calming visualization CD.
- Avoid heavy meals at bedtime; a light snack is okay.
- Avoid excessive fluid intake before bed.

- Eliminate alcohol, caffeine, and nicotine before bedtime.
- Prepare for bed every evening with "wind-down" time (e.g., bathing, brushing teeth, reading in comfortable chair, listening to soothing music).
- Create a nighttime environment with comfortable temperature, quietness, and darkness.
- Wear comfortable clothes to bed.
- If unable to fall asleep within 15-20 minutes, get out of bed and do a soothing activity (e.g., reading a calming book, watching a low-key movie) until you feel more tired, then try going back to sleep in your bed. If you can't fall asleep within 15-20 minutes, again get out of bed and do a soothing activity. You want to associate your bed with sleep, not tossing and turning.
- Do not label yourself as an insomniac or say things to yourself like "This is horrible, I'll never get a good night's sleep." Instead, try a statement like, "This is inconvenient, but I'll still function."
- Do not try to force yourself to fall asleep—this creates a type of performance anxiety in that you actually get the opposite of the desired effect. Paradoxically, many people fall asleep by trying to force themselves to stay awake.
- Try keeping a sleep diary (a sample is included in Appendix A) to detect patterns in what helps or hurts your sleep. If your sleep problems seem severe, ask your family doctor whether a consultation with a sleep specialist might be a good idea.

What type of self-talk can I use when I work myself up trying to fall asleep?

First of all, here are some examples of the kind of self-statements that work us up and make us more anxious:

- "I must have 8 hours of sleep."
- "I won't be able to function tomorrow at work."
- "Oh my gosh, it's already 4:00 a.m."

These self-statements increase your distress level and interfere with sleeping. Instead, try one of the self-statements below, or design your own. The most helpful attitude toward yourself is one of reassurance and soothing, like the way a good mother would soothe a child:

- "Everybody has a bad night now and then."
- "Even if I don't get as much sleep as I like, I'll still be able to function tomorrow."
- "I don't have to force myself to sleep—my body will sleep when it's ready to."
- "There are many people up working right now—I'm not the only one who is awake."

I become extremely anxious when I have to confront someone or say "no." I end up doing things I don't want to do just to avoid disappointing others. Why am I such a wimp?

It's doubtful you are a "wimp," but you may be communicating in a way that you think is protecting others. People who have trouble saying "no" often think in win-lose terms—one person wins and the other loses. If saying "no" feels like an aggressive defeat of the other person, it is understandable why you might avoid going there. Maybe you feel it's better to accept defeat yourself. People who prefer this outcome often communicate passively. You might be able to relate to this style:

Passive Communication:
- Does not express ideas directly
- Appears self-deprecating, apologetic
- Focuses on pleasing others
- Avoids conflict but doesn't get needs met
- Can result in disappointment and resentment

Message: You matter; I don't

Some people take the opposite stance, feeling they must win, and communicate aggressively. Here are the features of this approach:

Aggressive Communication:
- Expresses ideas in a domineering way
- Appears hostile or demanding
- Focuses on dominating, intimidating
- Produces desired results at others' expense
- Results in relationship problems

Message: I matter; you don't

There is another option available to you, a middle-ground option called *assertiveness*. Assertiveness takes into account your rights as well as the rights of others, encouraging negotiation rather than domination or submission. While assertiveness means honestly and directly expressing your desires, needs and opinions, it is not a guarantee that you will get your way. This is the tricky part. Sometimes people who don't like to say "no" also don't like it when others say "no"! Assertiveness involves room for "no" on both sides. However, asserting yourself and allowing others to do the same increases the chances for creative compromise and both parties getting what they want. Win-lose gets replaced by win-win. Here is what assertive communication looks like:

Assertive Communication:
- Expresses ideas directly
- Appears straightforward, confident
- Focuses on sharing information effectively
- Often produces desired results
- Can result in improved self-image *and* stronger relationships

Message: We both matter (equal rights)

Developing an assertive style of communication requires shifting some old beliefs and practicing new behaviors, but if it results in your getting more of what you want, less of what you don't want, and better relationships to boot, it's worth the effort!

My friends tell me it's no big deal if I say no or ask for what I want, but it is a big deal for me. Why is it so hard?

Difficulties in asserting yourself may arise from what you've come to believe about expressing your feelings. For example, if you were told you were "talking back" to your parents whenever you expressed your feelings, you might have learned that expressing yourself is rude. Your own temperament may be a factor as well. For example, if you are shy, you may have some general discomfort with telling others what you think and feel. Here are some other obstacles you may encounter when expressing yourself:

- Overestimation of danger, threat ("She'll hate me.")
- Underestimation of coping ("I'll feel terrible.")
- Memories of being criticized for expressing feelings
- Fear of rejection
- Intense emotions (too angry to speak)
- Regarding feelings as demands rather than preference

Regardless of the source of the problem, however, you can challenge old beliefs and assumptions and approach things with a fresh perspective. If it feels too hard to do on your own, seek out a therapist or an assertiveness training program to help and support you.

How do I keep from feeling uncomfortable when I want to tell someone "no" or ask for what I want?

First, let's look at what might be getting in the way. Here are some common beliefs that make it hard for us to express ourselves:

- Everyone must like me.
- I can't stand to make anybody mad.
- I couldn't bear to hurt her feelings.
- Saying something wouldn't do any good.
- It would be awful not to help him out.
- I can't say no.

Once you have a better sense of what is getting in the way, you can start to let go of old thinking and practice some new and more accurate ways of seeing things. Here are some examples of assertive thinking:

- It's okay for me to act in my best interests.
- I have a right to express my opinions.
- I don't control others' reactions, only my own.
- I'll help out when I can, but I don't have to feel obligated.
- Even if it's uncomfortable sometimes, I can say no.
- I can tolerate someone disagreeing with me.

Finally, as you practice new behaviors, be your own good coach. Here are some ways you can talk to yourself:

- This is hard now, but it will get easier with practice.
- I'm taking responsibility for my feelings. I can do this!

What are some daily activities I can schedule to reduce my anxiety?

One simple strategy is to schedule worry time. Surprised? This can actually be a great way to cut down on the amount of random worrying that you do throughout the day. You intentionally worry in a specified time and location to decrease on the amount of "spinning" that your mind does all day long. Here's how it works:

1. Schedule 15–30 minutes every day as a worry time and spend that time deliberately worrying.
2. At your worry time, write a list of your worries and focus intensely on each item. Really get into it.
3. If you find yourself worrying at other times – forcefully, actively tell yourself "I already thought about that in my worry time today" OR "I'll deal with that in my worry time tomorrow."
4. Over time, you will gain a more objective sense of your worries and be less troubled by these negative predictions. Your ability to fill up your worry time will gradually decrease. Keep in mind that being concerned and planning for the future is productive; excessive worrying, on the other hand, often keeps people stuck.

Throughout this book, the value of more helpful thinking and behaviors has been emphasized for better anxiety management. Appendix A contains several ideas for practicing new coping tools.

Appendix A: SELF-HELP TOOLS

My Distress Meter

Not all anxieties are created equal. Realizing this can help us feel calmer. Create your own distress meter by naming events in your life or imagination that correspond to the numerical level of distress. This will give you tangible benchmarks for tracking your anxiety level.

Level   **Event**

100 (worst feelings ever) _____

90 _____

80 _____

70 _____

60 _____

50 (moderate distress) _____

40 _____

30 _____

20 _____

10 _____

0 (no bad feelings) _____

Monitoring Anxiety Sequences

It helps to approach your anxiety as a detective. Note the situation where you become anxious, what you say to yourself about it, your anxiety level, and how you respond to the situation. This tracking will help you see the connections among your thoughts, feelings, and behaviors, thereby putting you in the driver's seat rather than your anxiety.

Situation	What I Tell Myself	Level of Anxiety (0–100)	Avoided Fear or Faced it?

Covering Both Bases

Remember that anxiety involves two thinking mistakes: 1) We over-estimate how dangerous or threatening the situation is, and 2) We underestimate our ability to cope with the situation. Use this work-sheet to record information that suggests the situation isn't as bad as you are thinking and that even if the worst happens, you'll be able to manage.

Adapted with permission from Thomas Ellis, PsyD, ABPP

This situation **might be okay.**	**Even if the worst happens, *I'll* be okay.**
Evidence: • • • •	Evidence: • • • •

Decision-Making Worksheet

Remember: There's no perfect decision, just choices with advantages and disadvantages. Which choice could you tolerate better or cope with more easily? Considering long-term benefits and costs (not just the short-term) is very important.

Choice A	
Advantages	**Disadvantages**

Choice B	
Advantages	**Disadvantages**

Challenging Negative Automatic Thoughts

Negative Automatic Thought: _____

Anxiety (0 = none 100 = most ever): _____

Behaviors: _____

What's the evidence that this thought is true? Not true?

_____

_____

What's another explanation? How else can I look at this?

_____

_____

Where is this thought getting me? Is it helping me or hurting me?

_____

_____

Is this thought a fact? Is this thought based on logic or emotional reasoning?

_____

_____

If my friend were in the situation and had this thought, what would I tell him or her?

_____

_____

What's the worst that could happen in this situation, and how would I deal with it?

_____

_____

Use this worksheet to reinforce the value of practicing more helpful self-talk.

Self-Talk Self-Help Worksheet

Situation: _____

_____

Anxious Self-Talk (What I'm telling myself or imagining:)	Anxious Feelings (0 = no anxiety 100 = most ever)
• • • •	• • • •

Coping Self-Talk (More realistic, balanced, helpful thoughts are:)	New Feelings (0 = no anxiety 100 = most ever)
• • • •	• • • •

Problem-Solving Worksheet

Given that you can't change the past and you can't predict the future, how can you address this problem now? Brainstorm, write down anything!

Specify the problem: _____		
Options for making it better	**Advantages of this option**	**Disadvantages of this option**
•	•	•
•	•	•
•	•	•
•	•	•

Which option looks most advantageous and least disadvantageous?

_____

Am I willing to try it?_____

How did it go when I tried this option? _____

_____

Am I satisfied with the results or do I want to consider another option?

_____

Remember that worrying can be an avoidance technique and tossing around "what ifs?" keeps you stuck. Use this worksheet to challenge your worry.

Stop and Think: Worry Worksheet

My worry is: _____

By *worrying* about this, will I:	Circle	
Keep the event from happening?	Yes	No
Figure out a way to avoid the problem?	Yes	No
Be prepared for the worst?	Yes	No
Be motivated to take action?	Yes	No
Can I be *keenly concerned* (instead of worried) and approach this as a problem to be managed?	Yes	No

What could I *think and do* to feel less upset and handle the problem better?

_____

_____

_____

Sleep Diary

Complete this worksheet each morning to gather data to improve your sleep habits.

	Sun	Mon	Tues	Wed	Thurs	Fri	Sat
Bedtime of previous night							
Rise time							
Estimated time to fall asleep							
Estimated number of awakenings							
Total time awake during night							
Estimated amount of sleep							
Any naps yesterday? Length?							
Rate how tired you feel*							
Rate irritability**							

*1 = wide awake   2 = fairly alert   3 = somewhat tired   4 = very tired

**1 = none   2 = some   3 = moderate   4= high

Progressive Muscle Relaxation

Progressive Muscle Relaxation is a well-researched and practiced relaxation technique. Systematically tensing and releasing muscle groups induces relaxation. Further, the practice of tensing and releasing helps you learn the difference between what a tight, tense muscle feels like and what a relaxed muscle feels like. Knowing this, you can identify and tell tense parts of your body to relax. In the following activity (adapted from Goldfried and Dawison, 1994), tightening the different muscle groups should create tension but never pain. You will tense and release each muscle group at least once, preferably twice, holding the tension for 5-10 seconds, then letting the muscle go limp for 15–20 seconds. Regular practice is key—try making your own audiotape of this script and using it daily.

Get comfortable in your chair (or bed) and begin to notice your breathing. Start to slow it down. Allow yourself to really appreciate how nice it feels to take slow, deep breaths. As you inhale, picture yourself breathing in calm. As you exhale, picture yourself breathing out tension.

Clench your left fist for 5–10 seconds. Hold. And now release for 15–20 seconds, letting your left hand rest comfortably, fingers loose. Notice how relaxed and loose your fingers feel.

Clench your right fist. Hold. Now release your right fist. Notice the difference between the tension and the relaxation. Really appreciate how nice it feels to have your fingers loose and relaxed.

Bend both hands back at the wrists so that your fingers are pointing toward the ceiling. Hold. Now release. Let your wrists rest, appreciating how relaxed they feel.

Tense your biceps by making fists and bringing your forearms up toward your shoulders. Pretend like you a doing a muscle man pose. Hold, feel the pulling, feel the tightness. And now release.

Now shrug your shoulders, raising them up as if to touch your ears. Feel the tension. Notice the tightness. Now release. Really notice the difference between what the tense muscles feel like and how comfortable it feels to have your shoulders relaxed and at ease.

Tense your triceps muscles by holding your arms straight out and locking your elbows. Hold. Feel the pulling. Study the tightness. And now release.

Tighten your forehead muscles by raising your eyebrows. Hold it, feel the pulling, feel the tightness. And now relax. Let your forehead become smooth and at ease. Notice how much nicer this feels.

Now tighten the muscles around your eyes by squeezing your eyelids shut. Hold, feel the pulling. Feel the tension. Now just relax and let go. See how nice it is to have the area around your eyes at ease.

Tighten your jaws by biting your teeth together. Bite down tightly, but without pain. Notice what it's like to feel your jaws clenched. Really appreciate the tightness, the tension. Now release. Let your lips part and notice the difference between the tension and the relaxation.

Tighten the muscles in the back of your neck by pressing your head back against the chair or the bed. Again do this to create tension but not pain. Most of us carry a lot of tension in our neck area. Feel what this tension and tightness are like. And now release. Enjoy the relaxed state of your head and neck resting comfortably.

Now arch your back. Stick out your chest and stomach. Pretend you are trying to touch your shoulder blades together. Hold the tension. Feel the pulling. Feel the tightness. Now release. Notice how nice it feels for that tightness to be replaced by relaxation.

Tense the muscles of your chest by taking in a deep breath. Hold it; hold it (about 10 seconds). Notice the chest muscles tightening. Feel the pulling. And now release. Let yourself enjoy how nice it feels to exhale and let that chest tension go. Picture tension leaving your body through that breath. Many of us hold our breath during times of stress. Really appreciate what it's like to breath regularly and comfortably.

Tense your stomach muscles by holding your stomach in as if you are trying to touch the back of the chair or bed. Suck your stomach in. Hold it. Feel the tension. Notice the tightness. And now release. See how nice it is to let go of that tension in your stomach muscles.

Now tense the muscles in your thighs all the way down to your knees by stretching both legs out. Stretch your legs. Point your toes. Feel the pulling. Notice the tightness. Pretend you are trying to make your thigh muscles very tight and hard. And now release. Let yourself see how pleasant it feels to have these large muscles at ease. Enjoy how relaxed these big muscles feel.

Tense your calf muscles by pulling your toes toward you. Hold, tighten. Feel the pulling. Notice the tightness. And now release. Enjoy the relaxation spreading through your calves and your entire legs.

Now that you've tightened and relaxed your major muscle groups, scan your body to see if there is any tension remaining and release it. Enjoy the relaxed, calm feeling that is present throughout your body.

Visualizations

To help with relaxation you can make an audiotape of the following visualizations, or purchase one that captures the setting that appeals to you:

Outdoor scene

Imagine an autumn sunny day when the air is fresh and crisp. The sky is bright blue with only a few billowy white clouds. The temperature is a very comfortable 60 degrees and you long to be outside. You decide to take a walk through the park. You put on a light jacket and you head toward the park. A pleasant breeze brushes your face, and you enjoy seeing the changing colors of the leaves on the trees. Look how beautiful the hues are—bright yellows, reds, and oranges—almost like confetti in the sky. Many of the leaves have fallen to the ground, and some crinkle under your feet on the grass. You like this autumn sound and notice yourself beginning to feel very calm and peaceful. You find that you enjoy watching the children play on the swings and the merry-go-round. It's nice to see them laughing and making the most of the day.

As you're walking through the park, you notice a path into the woods. You see a clear trail and decide to take it. It begins to get a little darker as you walk along the path with the trees providing more of a ceiling for you. Look up and see the oak, pine, and fir trees. Marvel at how large some of these trees are and appreciate how long they have been here. See their massive trunks and appreciate how their intricate branches form a web covering the blue sky. Become aware now of how many of the leaves have fallen to the ground. As you walk, you hear more dried leaves and small twigs cracking, but it's a very pleasant sound to you. You enjoy the feel of the leaves under your feet as you go deeper along the trail. You continue walking, noting that it's getting a little cooler as the sun is more blocked out by the trees. Cooler sensations are spreading through your body. You can smell the earth more as you walk through the woods. Progressing deeper into the forest, you're feeling calmer and really noticing that a sense of tranquility is spreading through your body. It's as if you can put all your concerns aside as you enjoy the beautiful portrait that Mother Nature has provided.

Beach

On this beautiful cloudless day, with a radiant blue sky, you decide to go to the beach. You walk through the high grass over to the narrow boardwalk. You decide to leave your shoes on the top of the platform. As you walk down to the shore, you feel increasingly pleasant in anticipation of reaching the sand. Looking out, you feel in awe of the beauty and magnitude of the beach. It extends as far off as you can see. The white sand is very fine and shimmers like crystals in the sun. It is exhilarating to step down and feel the sand between your toes as you walk. Really notice the warm gritty feeling of the sand, how good this sensation feels on this glorious summer day. Even the pounding surf brings such serenity to your mind when you see the waves come in and go out. The blue of the water is so bright and vivid that the ocean just seems to glisten. Calmness and relaxation spread through your body as you continue to take in these beach sights. The smell of the fresh salt air only seems to intensify that calmness. The sounds of birds flying over you, the heat of the sun on your body, and the breeze blowing from the water are even more soothing. Thinking of how glorious the beach looks and how beautiful the day is, you are drawn to stay here for a while. As you sit down and eventually lie back, you are overwhelmed by the comfort of the sand, and tranquility continues to build in you. You find yourself sinking into an even deeper state of relaxation. Feeling the sunshine on your face…hearing the surf and the continuous cycle of waves coming in and going out. All of these beach sensations produce a very soothing sense of calm in your body. Allow yourself to feel the joy of being on the beach, just appreciating the beauty of nature.

Pleasure Menu

Having times and ways to enjoy yourself not only feels good, but rejuvenates you to face life's stressors. Different people benefit from different activities—the key here is to pick something you can enjoy and commit to doing the activity regularly. Circle the self-care activities you would like to incorporate in your life.

walking	taking a drive in a	watering plants
writing a letter	pretty area	getting a facial
getting a massage	sex	running
listening to pleasant	scrapbooking	lighting candles
music	cooking	praying
calling a friend	singing	doing a relaxation
reading your child a	sewing	exercise
story	going to church	yoga
meeting a friend for	gardening	dancing
coffee	lifting weights	looking at fall leaves
getting a	fishing	babysitting
manicure/pedicure	going to a ballet or	arranging flowers
going to a movie	sports event	working in the
planning a vacation	bird-watching	garage
taking a bubble bath	going out for ice	washing the car
journaling	cream	framing pictures
going to the gym	hiking	hugging a family
reading a good book	washing the car	member
visiting a relative	photography	tennis
joining a book club	playing with a pet	golf
shopping (as long as	throwing Frisbee	wood-working
you're not over-	volunteering	meditation
spending)	needlework	cooking
swimming	painting	watching television
asking your spouse	drawing	
for a back rub	doing crafts	

Other ideas? _____

_____

Activity Monitor

A balance of work and leisure is important for anxiety management. Try using the following Activity Monitor below to get an overview of how you are spending your time. Use the first page to note how you spend each hour of a typical day:

- Is your time consumed by work and obligations?
- Is almost every hour busy? How much sleep are you getting?
- How much time, if any, do you spend on pleasurable activities?

Now use the second page to plan how you'd *like* your day to go:

- What are your top priorities, and how do you assure you get these done?
- Where can you schedule "down time" and pleasurable activities?
- What responsibilities can you delegate to other family members?

You can also rate your level of enjoyment for the activities you are doing (0 = no enjoyment at all, 10 = most enjoyment ever). Note how your stress level fluctuates with your level of enjoyment.

Activity Monitor: Actual Day

Time	Mon	Tues	Wed	Thurs	Fri	Sat	Sun
7 am							
8 am							
9 am							
10 am							
11 am							
12 noon							
1 pm							
2 pm							
3 pm							
4 pm							
5 pm							
6 pm							
7 pm							
8 pm							
9 pm							
10 pm							
11 pm							
12 midnight							
1 am–7 am							

Activity Monitor: Ideal Day

Time	Mon	Tues	Wed	Thurs	Fri	Sat	Sun
7 am							
8 am							
9 am							
10 am							
11 am							
12 noon							
1 pm							
2 pm							
3 pm							
4 pm							
5 pm							
6 pm							
7 pm							
8 pm							
9 pm							
10 pm							
11 pm							
12 midnight							
1 am–7 am							

Appendix B RESOURCES

Books

Adams, K. A. (1990). *Journal To The Self.* Warner Books.

American Psychiatric Association. (1994). *Diagnostic and Statistical Manual of Mental Disorders—4th edition.* Washington, DC: Author.

Barlow, D. H. & Craske, M. G. (1994). *Mastery of Your Anxiety and Panic II.* Albany, New York: Graywind Publications.

Basco, M. R. (1999). *Never Good Enough: How to Use Perfectionism to Your Advantage without Letting it Ruin Your Life.* New York: Simon & Schuster.

Beck, A. T. (1976). *Cognitive Therapy and the Emotional Disorders.* New York: Penguin Books USA Inc.

Beck, A. T. (1988). *Love Is Never Enough.* New York: Harper & Row Publishers, Inc.

Beck, A. T., Emery, G., & Greenberg, R. L. (1985). *Anxiety Disorders and Phobias: A Cognitive Perspective.* New York: Basic Books.

Beck, J. (1995). *Cognitive Therapy: Basics and Beyond.* (1995). New York: The Guilford Press.

Bourne, Edmund, PhD. (1995). *The Anxiety and Phobia Workbook (2nd Edition).* New Harbinger Publications.

Bower, S. A., & Bower, G. H. (1991). *Asserting Yourself: A Practical Guide for Positive Change: Updated Edition.* Reading, Massachusetts: Addison-Wesley Publishing Company.

Burns, D. D. (1985). *Intimate Connections.* New York: A Signet Book, New American Library.

Burns, D. D. (1989). *The Feeling Good Handbook.* New York: Penguin Books USA Inc.

Chansky, T. E. (2000). *Freeing Your Child from Obsessive-Compulsive Disorder.* New York: Three Rivers Press.

Ciarrocchi, J. W. (1995). *The Doubting Disease: Help for Scrupulosity and Religious Compulsions.* New York: Paulist Press.

Copeland, M. E. (1998). *The Worry Control Workbook.* Oakland, California: New Harbinger Publications, Inc.

Craske, M. G., Barlow, D. H., & O'Leary, T. (1992). *Mastery of Your Anxiety and Worry.* Albany, New York: Graywind Publications.

Davis, M., Eshelman, E. R., & McKay, M. (1995). *The Relaxation and Stress Reduction Workbook: Fourth Edition.* Oakland, California: New Harbinger Publications, Inc.

Ellis, A. (1998). *How to Control Your Anxiety Before It Controls You.* New York: Kensington Publishing Corporation.

Foa, E. B., & Wilson, R. (2001). *Stop Obsessing! How to Overcome Your Obsessions and Compulsions.* Bantam.

Freeman, A, & DeWolf, R. (1992). *The 10 Dumbest Mistakes Smart People Make and How to Avoid Them: Simple and Sure Techniques for Gaining Greater Control of Your Life.* New York: HarperCollins Publishers, Inc.

Garber, S. W., Garber, M. D., & Spizman, R. F. (1993). *Monsters Under the Bed and Other Childhood Fears: Helping Your Child Overcome Anxieties, Fears, and Phobias.* New York: Villard Books.

Goldfried, M.R., & Davison, G.C. (1994). *Clinical Behavior Therapy: Expanded Edition.* New York: John Wiley and Sons, Inc.

Granet, R. & McNally, R. A. (1998). *If You Think You Have Panic Disorder (A Dell Mental Health Guide).*

Greenberger, D., & Padesky, C. A. (1995). *Mind Over Mood: Change How You Feel by Changing the Way You Think.* New York: The Guilford Press.

Helgoe, L. (2004) *Boomer's Guide to Dating (Again).* New York: Alpha Books.

Kabat-Zinn, J. (1990). *Full Catastrophe Living: Using the Wisdom of Your Body and Mind to Face Stress, Pain, and Illness.* New York: A Delta Book, Dell Publishing.

Levine, P. A. (1997). *Waking the Tiger: Healing Trauma.* California: North Atlantic Books.

Pennebaker, J. W. *Opening Up: The Healing Power of Expressing Emotions.* New York: Guilford Press.

Penzel, F. (2000). *Obsessive-Compulsive Disorders—A Complete Guide to Getting Well and Staying Well.* New York: Oxford University Press.

Peurifoy, R. Z. (1988). *Anxiety, Phobias, and Panic: A Step-by-Step Program for Regaining Control of Your Life.* New York: Warner Books, Inc.

Rapoport, J. (1997). *The Boy Who Couldn't Stop Washing: The Experience and Treatment of Obsessive-Compulsive Disorder.* New York: Signet Books.

Ross, J. (1994). *Triumph Over Fear: A Book of Help and Hope for People with Anxiety, Panic Attacks, and Phobias.* New York: Bantam.

Schwartz, J. M. (1996). *Brain Lock.* New York: Regan Books.

Shay, J. (1994). *Achilles in Vietnam: Combat Trauma and the Undoing of Character.* New York: Scribner.

Steketee, G. S. & White, K. (1990*). When Once Is Not Enough: Help for Obsessive Compulsives.* Oakland, CA: New Harbinger Publications.

Weekes, Claire. (1991). *Help and Hope for Your Nerves.* New York: Signet Books.

Wilson, R. Reid, PhD. (1987). *Don't panic: Taking control of anxiety attacks.* New York: Harper Perennial Publishers.

Young, J. E. & Klosko, J. S. (1994). *Reinventing Your Life: The Breakthrough Program to End Negative Behavior...and Feel Great Again.* New York: Plume Books.

Zuercher-White, E. (1995). *An End To Panic: Break Through Techniques For Overcoming Panic Disorder.* Oakland, CA: New Harbinger Publications.

Websites

The Academy of Cognitive Therapy: www.acadamyofct.org
Albert Ellis Institute: www.rebt.org
American Academy of Child and Adolescent Psychiatry: www.aacap.org
American Psychiatric Association: www.healthyminds.org
American Psychiatric Association: www.psych.org
American Psychological Association: www.ape.org
Anxiety Disorders Association of America: www.adaa.org
Association for the Advancement of Behavior Therapy: www.aabt.org
The Beck Institute for Cognitive Therapy and Research: www.beckinstitute.org
ChildTrauma Academy: www.childtrauma.org
Fredd Culbertson's list of phobias: www.phobialist.com
Freedom From Fear: www.freedomfromfear.com
National Center for PTSD: www.ncptsd.org
National Center for Victims of Crime: www.ncvc.org
National Institute of Mental Health: www.nimh.nih.gov
National Mental Health Association: www.nmha.org
National Sexual Violence Resource Center: www.nsvrc.org
The Obsessive-Compulsive Disorder Foundation, Inc.: www.ocfoundation.org
R. Reid Wilson, Ph.D: www.anxieties.com

Index

About the Authors

Laurie A. Helgoe, PhD, is a clinical psychologist with over 15 years of experience, and a nationally recognized relationship expert. She practices at Family Psychiatric Services in Charleston, West Virginia, where she provides psychological assessment and diagnosis, psychotherapy, and consultation. Dr. Helgoe is author of the *Boomer's Guide to Dating (Again)*, published in 2004 by Penguin Group/Alpha, and is a columnist and frequent talk show guest. She provides teaching and consultation at the undergraduate, graduate, and postgraduate levels, and offers consultation, lectures, and workshops to new and practicing clinicians, as well as to the general public. Dr. Helgoe can be reached at *www.wakingdesire.com*.

Laura R. Wilhelm, PhD, received her doctoral degree in Clinical Psychology from Ohio University in 2000. She works as an Assistant Professor at the Department of Behavioral Medicine and Psychiatry at the Robert C. Byrd Health Sciences Center, West Virginia University School of Medicine in Charleston, West Virginia. Her outpatient practice focuses on the treatment of anxiety disorders, depression, and anger problems in adults. Other clinical interests include adjustment to medical problems, stress management, assertiveness, and group therapy. Dr. Wilhelm also serves as the Director of her department's Cognitive-Behavioral Therapy Training Program, in which she teaches and supervises psychiatric residents, psychology interns, and medical students.

Martin J. Kommor, MD, is Chair of the Department of Behavioral Medicine and Psychiatry at the Robert C. Byrd Health Sciences Center of the West Virginia University School of Medicine, in Charleston, West Virginia, where he has taught for almost 30 years. In addition to teaching, Dr. Kommor provides psychotherapy and medication consultation, conducts research, and is active in mental health and psychiatric associations. He has also provided stress debriefing to community and state paramedics, firemen, and police. A psychodynamically-oriented psychiatrist, Dr. Kommor emphasizes to students that patients with psychiatric illness "are always unique people, and never just a disease or set of symptoms to be medicated away."